EDWARD BOND

Saved

METHUEN DRAMA

Methuen Modern Plays

3 5 7 9 10 8 6 4

First published in 1966 by
Methuen and Co. Ltd

This edition published in 2000 by
Methuen Publishing Limited
215 Vauxhall Bridge Road, London SW1V 1EJ

Copyright © 1965, 2000 by Edward Bond

Methuen Publishing Limited Reg. No. 3543167

A CIP catalogue record for this book
is available from the British Library

ISBN 0 413 31360 3

Printed and bound in Great Britain by
Cox & Wyman Ltd, Reading, Berkshire

Caution

The Methuen Modern Plays series has always been at the forefront of modern playwriting. Since 1959, the series has reflected the most exciting developments in modern drama, making the most significant plays widely available in paperback.

Saved

After a licence for public performance had been refused by the Lord Chamberlain, Saved was first staged in November 1965 at the Royal Court Theatre before a 'members only' audience of the English Stage Society. It quickly became the subject of fierce debate and has passed into the international repertoire of the modern theatre.

'Saved is a study of reduction of personality that makes no excuses and offers no kicks, executed with a hard-headed humanity and a brazen technique'

Penelope Gilliatt, The Observer

'Saved is not for children but it is for grown-ups, and the grown-ups of this country should have the courage to look at it'

Sir Laurence Olivier in a letter to The Observer

Edward Bond was born and educated in London. His plays include The Pope's Wedding (Royal Court Theatre, 1962); Saved (Royal Court, 1965); Early Morning (Royal Court, 1968); Narrow Road to the Deep North (Belgrade Theatre, Coventry, 1968; Royal Court, 1969); Black Mass (Sharpeville Commemoration Evening, Lyceum Theatre, 1970); Passion (CND Rally, Alexandra Palace, 1971); Lear (Royal Court, 1971); The Sea (Royal Court, 1973); Bingo (Northcott, Exeter, 1973; Royal Court 1974); The Fool (Royal Court, 1975); We Come to the River (Covent Garden Opera, 1976); The Bundle (RSC Warehouse, 1978); The Woman (National Theatre, 1978); The Worlds (New Half Moon Theatre, London, 1981); Restoration (Royal Court, 1981); Summer (National Theatre, 1982); Derek (RSC Youth Festival, The Other Place, Stratford-upon-Avon, 1982); The Cat (produced in Germany as The English Cat by the Stuttgart Opera, 1983); Human Cannon (Quantum Theatre, Manchester, 1986); The War Plays (Red Black and Ignorant, The Tin Can People and Great Peace) (RSC, Barbican, 1985; Odéon Théâtre, Paris, 1995); Jackets (Haymarket, Leicester, 1989); September (Canterbury Cathedral, 1989); In the Company of Men (Théâtre de la Ville, Paris, 1992; RSC Barbican 1996); At the Inland Sea (toured by Big Brum Theatre-in-Education, 1995); Eleven Vests (toured by Big Brum Theatre-in-Education, 1997); Olly's Prison (BBC2 TV, 1993; Berliner Ensemble, Germany, 1994); Tuesday (BBC Schools TV, 1993; Théâtre de la Colline, Paris, 1994); The Children (Classworks, Cambridge, 2000); Coffee (Théâtre de la Colline, Paris, 2000) and The Crime of the Twenty-First Century (Théâtre de la Colline, Paris, 2000). His Theatre Poems and Songs were published in 1978; Poems 1978–1985 in 1987 and The Edward Bond Letters (vols. 1–5) in 1994, 1995, 1996, 1998, and 2000; Chair (BBC Radio 4, 2000).

by the same author

in Methuen's Modern Plays
A-A-AMERICA! & STONE
HUMAN CANNON
LEAR
OLLY'S PRISON
SAVED
THE SEA
TWO POST-MODERN PLAYS:
(Jackets, In the Company of Men, September)
THE WAR PLAYS:
(Red Black and Ignorant, The Tin Can People, Great Peace)

in the World Classics Series
PLAYS: ONE
(Saved, Early Morning, The Pope's Wedding)
PLAYS: TWO
(Lear, The Sea, Narrow Road to the Deep North,
Black Mass, Passion)
PLAYS: THREE
(Bingo, The Fool, The Woman)
PLAYS: FOUR
(The Worlds *with* The Activists Papers, Restoration, Summer)
PLAYS: FIVE
(Human Cannon, The Bundle, Jackets, In the Companay of Men)
PLAYS: SIX
(The War Plays, Choruses from After the Assassinations)

Poetry
THEATRE POEMS AND SONGS
POEMS 1978–1985

also available

Translated by Edward Bond and
Elisabeth Bond-Pablé

WEDEKIND PLAYS: ONE
(Spring Awakening, Lulu: A Monster Tragedy)

Author's Note

Saved is almost irresponsibly optimistic. Len, the chief character, is good in spite of his upbringing and environment, but he is not wholly or easily good because then his goodness would be meaningless, at least for himself.

It is true that at the end of the play Len does not know what he will do next, but then he never has done. The play ends in silent social stalemate, but if audiences think this is pessimistic that is because they have not learned to clutch at straws. Clutching at straws is the only realistic thing to do. The alternative, apart from the self-indulgence of pessimism, is a fatuous optimism. The gesture of turning the other cheek is often a way of refusing to look facts in the face. This is not true of Len. He lives with people at their most hopeless (that is the point of the final scene) and does not turn away from them. I cannot imagine an optimism more tenacious or honest than this.

By not playing his traditional role in the play's tragic Oedipal pattern, Len turns it into what is formally a comedy. The Oedipal outcome should be a quarrel and death. There is a quarrel and even a struggle with a knife – but Len continues to try to understand and help. The next scene starts with him stretched on the floor with a knife in his hand and the old man comes in dressed as a ghost. But neither of them is dead. The only sensible object in defeating an enemy is to make him your friend.

Clearly the stoning to death of a baby in a London park is a typical English understatement. Compared to the 'strategic' bombing of cities it is a negligible atrocity. Compared to the cultural and emotional deprivation of most children its consequences are insignificant.

Almost all morality taught to children is grounded in religion. This in itself bewilders them – religion has nothing to do with their parents' personal lives, or our economic, industrial and political life, and is contrary to the science and reason they are taught at other times. For them religion discredits the morality it is meant to sustain. The result is that they grow up morally illiterate and cannot understand, because they have not been taught, the nature of a moral consideration or the value of morals at all. This is not always noticed because we use words that still have moral connotations, but these are being lost. Morals cannot be slapped on as a social lubricant. They must share a common basis with social organisation and be consistent with accepted knowledge. That means teaching understanding not faith.

Like most people I am a pessimist by experience but an optimist by nature. I shall go on being true to my nature. It is often a mistake to learn from experience.

Saved

SAVED was first presented by the English Stage Company at the Royal Court Theatre, London, on 3rd November, 1965, with the following cast:

LEN, twenty-one. Tall, slim, firm, bony. Big hands. High, sharp cheekbones. Pleasant pale complexion – not ashen. Blue eyes, thick fair hair a bit oily, brushed sideways from a parting. Prominent feet.

John Castle

FRED, twenty-one. Blond, very curly hair. Medium height. Well-shaped, steady, powerful body. Light tenor voice.

Tony Selby

HARRY, sixty-eight. Tall. Long thin arms. Long hands. Heavy, bony head with large eye-sockets and small eyes. Loose chin. Grey.

Richard Butler

PETE, twenty-five. Tallish. Well-built, red-faced. Makes very few gestures. Soft hair that tends to stick up lightly.

Ronald Pickup

COLIN, shortish. A bit thin. Loose (but not big) mouth. Shiny ears, curved featureless face. A few spots. Shouts to make himself heard. Eighteen.

Dennis Waterman

MIKE, tall. Well-built. Strong, easy, emphatic movements. Pleasant. Dark hair. Twenty.

John Bull

BARRY, twenty. A little below medium height. Fat.

William Stewart

PAM, twenty-three. Thin, sharp-busted. Heavy, nodal hips. Dark hair. Long narrow face. Pale eyes. Small mouth. Looks tall from a distance, but is shorter than she looks.

Barbara Ferris

MARY, fifty-three. Shortish. Round heavy shoulders. Big buttocks. Bulky breasts, lifeless but still high. Big thighs and little ankles. Curled grey hair that looks as if it is in a hair-net. Homely.

Gwen Nelson

LIZ, exactly as she sounds.   *Alison Frazer*

Directed by William Gaskill
Assistant to Director Jane Howell
Designed by John Gunter
Stage Manager Juliet Alliston
Assistant to Stage Manager Allison Rockley

Scene one	Living-room	Scene eight	Living-room
Scene two	Park	Scene nine	Living-room
Scene three	Park	Scene ten	Café
Scene four	Living-room	Scene eleven	Living-room
Scene five	Bedroom	Scene twelve	Bedroom
Scene six	Park	Scene thirteen	Living-room
Scene seven	Cell		

The area of the play is South London

The stage is as bare as possible – sometimes completely bare.

There should be an interval after Scene Seven.

SCENE ONE

The living-room. The front and the two side walls make a triangle that slopes to a door back centre.

Furniture: table down right, sofa left, TV set left front, armchair up right centre, two chairs close to the table.

Empty.

The door opens. Len comes in. He goes straight out again.

PAM (*off*). In there.

LEN *comes in. He goes down to the sofa. He stares at it.*

All right?

Pause. PAM *comes in.*

LEN. This ain' the bedroom.
PAM. Bed ain' made.
LEN. Oo's bothered?
PAM. It's awful. 'Ere's nice.
LEN. Suit yourself. Yer don't mind if I take me shoes off? (*He kicks them off.*) No one 'ome?
PAM. No.
LEN. Live on yer tod?
PAM. No.
LEN. O.

Pause. He sits back on the couch.

Yer all right? Come over 'ere.
PAM. In a minit.
LEN. Wass yer name?
PAM. Yer ain' arf nosey.

LEN. Somethin' up?

PAM. Can't I blow me nose?

*She puts her hanky back in her bag and puts it on the table.
Better.*

She sits on the couch.

LEN. Wass yer name?

PAM. Wass yourn?

LEN. Len.

PAM. Pam.

LEN. O. (*He feels the couch behind with his hand.*) This big
   enough?

PAM. What yer want? Bligh!

LEN. Don't wan' a push yer off. Shove that cushion up.

PAM. 'Ang on.

LEN. 'Ow often yer done this?

PAM. Don't be nosey.

LEN. Take yer shoes off.

PAM. In a minit.

LEN. Can yer move yer – thass better.

PAM. Yer d'narf fidget.

LEN. I'm okay now.

PAM. Ow!

LEN. D'yer 'ave the light on?

PAM. Suit yerself.

LEN. I ain' fussy.

PAM. Ow!

LEN. Can yer shut them curtains?

PAM *goes left to the curtains.*

   Yer got a fair ol'arse.

PAM. Like your mug.

LEN. Know somethin'? – I ain' touched a tart for weeks.

PAM. Don't know what yer missin'.

LEN. Don't I?

PAM *sits on the couch, on the edge.* LEN *pulls her closer and takes off her shoes.*

Lucky.

PAM. What?

LEN. Bumpin' in t'you.

PAM. Yeh.

LEN. Yer don't mind me?

PAM. No.

LEN. Sure?

PAM. Yer wan'a get on with it.

LEN. Give us a shout if I do somethin' yer don't reckon.

PAM. Bligh! Yer ain' better 'ave.

LEN. I could go for you. Know that?

Pause.

This is the life.

PAM. Ow!

LEN. Sh! Keep quiet now.

PAM. Oi!

LEN. Sh!

PAM. Yer told me t'shout!

The door opens. HARRY *comes in. He goes straight out again.*

LEN (*lifts his head*). 'Ere!

PAM. What?

LEN. Oo's that?

PAM. Ol' man.

LEN (*sits*). Whass 'e want?

PAM. That cushion's stickin' in me back.

LEN. I thought yer reckon yer was on yer tod?

PAM. 'E's late for work.

LEN. O. Why?

PAM. Why?

LEN. Yeh.

PAM. I don't know.

LEN. Reckon 'e saw?

PAM. Shouldn't be surprised.

LEN. Will 'e be long?

PAM. Don't arst me.

LEN. O. Well.

They lie down again. Slight pause. LEN *lifts his head.*

'Ear that?

PAM. No.

LEN. I 'eard somethin'.

He goes to the door. He listens. He goes back to the couch and sits on the end.

PAM. Well?

LEN. Better 'ang on.

PAM. Why?

LEN. Better 'ad.

PAM. Think yer'll last?

LEN. Not if yer lie around like that.

PAM. Like what?

LEN. Sit up.

PAM. I juss got right.

LEN. More'n I 'ave. Chriss. (*He feels in his pocket.*) You smoke?

PAM. In me bag.

LEN. Where's yer bag?

PAM *nods at the table. He goes to the bag and takes out a cigarette. He lights it. He starts putting the cigarettes back.*

Oh, sorry.

He holds the packet out to her.

PAM. No thanks.

LEN (*he puts the cigarettes away. He sits on the edge of the*

couch. Pause. He taps his foot three or four times). **Wass**
'is caper?

PAM. Wan'a cup 'a tea?

LEN. After.

PAM. 'E won't be long.

LEN. 'Adn't better. 'Ave a puff?

PAM. No.

LEN. Do yer dress up.

PAM. Sorry.

LEN. Yer never know 'oo's poppin' in.

He goes to the door and opens it.

PAM. You off?

LEN. I could'a swore I 'eard 'eavy breathin'.

PAM. Thass you.

LEN. 'Oo else yer got knockin' about? Yer ain't stuffed yer
grannie under the sofa?

PAM. She's dead.

LEN. 'Ard luck. – Wass 'is caper?

He sits on a chair.

My blinkin' luck.

He stands and walks.

'E'll be late, won't 'e! I 'ope they dock 'is bloody packet.

He listens by the door.

Not a twitter.

PAM. 'E ain' bin out the back yet.

LEN. The ol' twit.

PAM *laughs.*

Wass the joke?

PAM. You.

LEN (*amused*). Yeh. Me. Ha! 'E's a right ol' twit, ain' 'e!
'Ere, can I stay the night?

PAM. Ain' yer got nowhere?

LEN. Yeh! – Well?

PAM. No.

LEN. Yer're the loser. – Sure's 'e's goin'? – Why can't I?

PAM. Bligh! I only juss met yer.

LEN. Suppose 'e's stoppin' 'ome? Got a cold or somethin'.
I'd do me nut! – Yer'd enjoy it.

PAM. Big 'ead.

LEN. 'Ow many blokes yer 'ad this week?

PAM. We ain't finished Monday yet!

LEN. We'll take that into consideration.

PAM. Saucy bugger!

They laugh.

'Ow many times yer 'ad it this week?

LEN. I told yer once! 'Ow many blokes yer 'ad all told?

They laugh.

PAM. What about you an' girls?

LEN. Can't count over sixty.

They laugh.

PAM. Sh!

LEN. 'E'll 'ear. – Oi, tell us!

PAM. 'Ow many times yer done it in one night?

They laugh.

LEN. Why did the woman with three tits shoot 'erself?

PAM. Eh?

LEN. She only 'ad two nipples.

They laugh.

PAM. I don't get it. (*She laughs.*) What did the midwife say to the nun?

LEN. Don' know.

She whispers in his ear. They laugh.

You're great! What about the woman with three tits 'oo 'ad quads?

PAM. Eh?

LEN. That'll teach 'er t'sleep with siamese twins!

They laugh. He whispers in her ear.

PAM. Yer ought a be locked up!

LEN. That's a feedin' problem!

PAM. Sh – thass the back door. 'E's bin out the lav.

LEN. Less give 'im a thrill.

He jumps noisily on the couch.

Cor – blimey!

PAM. You're terrible!

He takes some sweets from her bag.

They're my sweets.

LEN. Less 'ave a choose. (*Loudly.*) 'Ow's that for size?

PAM. What yer shoutin?

LEN (*he puts a sweet in her mouth*). Go easy! Yer wanna make it last!

She laughs. He bites a sweet in half and looks at it.

Oo, yer got a lovely little soft centre.
(*Aside to* PAM). First time I seen choclit round it!

He jumps on the sofa.

PAM (*shrill*). Yer awful!

LEN. That still 'ard?

PAM (*laughs*). Leave off!

LEN. Come on, there's plenty more where that come from.

He puts a sweet in her mouth.

PAM (*splutters*). Can't take no more!

LEN. Yeh – open it. Yer can do a bit more!

PAM. Ow!

LEN. Oorr lovely!

He tickles her. She chokes.

This'll put 'airs on yer chest!

They try to laugh quietly. The door opens. HARRY *puts his head in. He goes out. He shuts the door.* LEN *calls:*

'Ave a toffee!

PAM. Oo-oo 'ave a toffee!

LEN. Tried that mint with the 'ole in it?

PAM. 'Ave a toffee!

LEN. What about the ol' dolly mixture? – Will 'e give yer a ruckin'?

PAM. Ain' got the nerve.

LEN (*calls*). Nosey ol' gander!

They laugh.

See 'is tongue 'angin' out?

PAM. 'E's fetchin' 'is dinner-box out the kitchen.

LEN (*calls*). Don't work too 'ard, mate!

PAM. Lay off, or 'e'll stay in out a spite.

LEN (*calls*). Take a toffee for tea break, Dad! – I'd like'a sleep round 'ere. Yer'd be lovely an' warm in the mornin'.

PAM. Yer're juss greedy!

LEN. I give yer 'alf the sweets!

PAM. I paid. Anyway, Mum'll be back.

LEN. O. That the front door?

PAM. Yeh.

She goes to the curtains.

'E's off.

LEN. Didn't take long.

PAM. I tol' yer.

LEN. Better be worth waitin' for.

PAM. Up to you, ain' it!

LEN. Thass all right then.

She comes to the sofa and starts to undo his belt.

This is the life.

SCENE TWO

Park.

PAM *and* LEN *in a rowing boat. Otherwise stage bare.*

LEN. Cold?

PAM. No.

LEN. Still pecky?

PAM. Yeh.

LEN. There's a bit'a choclit left. 'Ere.

PAM. No.

LEN. Go on.

PAM. Ta.

LEN. Thass yer lot.

PAM. Why?

LEN. No more.

Silence.

I still ain' paid me rent this week.

PAM. Me mum won't reckon that.

LEN. Ain' got round to it.

PAM. Surprised she ain' said.

Slight pause.

LEN. She ever let on?

PAM. 'Bout us?

LEN. Yeh.

PAM. No.

LEN. She don't mind?

PAM. Don't 'ave to. Your money comes in 'andy.

Silence.

LEN. She reckon me, yer reckon?

PAM. Never arst.

LEN. Thought she might'a said.

PAM. Never listen.

LEN. O.

PAM. Yer ain't spent it?

LEN. 'Er rent?

PAM. Yeh.

LEN. Nah!

PAM. Juss wondered.

LEN. Don' yer truss me?

PAM. I'm goin' a knit yer a jumper.

LEN. For me?

PAM. I ain' very quick.

LEN. Can't say I noticed.

PAM. Yer'll 'ave t'buy the wool.

LEN. Knew there'd be a catch.

PAM. I got a smashin' pattern.

LEN. You worried about that rent?

PAM. I 'ad it give us.

LEN. Yer 'adn't better be one of them naggers.

PAM. What colour's best?

LEN. Thass about one thing your ol' girl *don't* do.

PAM. What?

LEN. Nag 'er ol' man.

PAM. What's yer best colour?

LEN. They all suit me.

PAM. I like a red. Or a blue.

LEN. Anythin' bright.

Slight pause.

PAM. I 'ave t' 'ave an easy pattern.

LEN. Will it be ready for the 'oneymoon?

PAM. We ain' 'avin' 'oneymoon.

LEN. 'Oo's payin'?

PAM. You.

LEN. I can see I'll 'ave t' watch out.

Pause.

PAM. Whass the time?

LEN. Don't know.

PAM. Gettin' on.

LEN. Shouldn't wonder.

PAM. Where's the choclit?

LEN. Yer 'ad it all.

PAM. O.

LEN. Sorry.

PAM. There weren't much.

LEN. I'll get some when we go in.

PAM. I 'ad a blinkin' great dinner.

LEN. I reckon yer got a kid on the way.

PAM. I ain'.

LEN. Never know yer luck.

PAM. Yer'll 'ave t' get up early in the mornin' t' catch me.

LEN. Done me best.

PAM. Yer got a dirty mind.

Slight pause.

LEN. I'm 'andy with me 'ands. Yer know, fix up the ol'
decoratin' lark and knock up a few things. Yeh. We'll 'ave
a fair little place. I ain' livin' in no blinkin' sty.

PAM. Sounds all right.

LEN. Easy t' kep swep' out an' that. Yer'll be all right.

PAM. I'd better.

He puts his head in her lap. There is a slight pause.

LEN. 'S great 'ere.

Pause.

Pam.

PAM. What?

LEN. Why did yer pick me up like that?

PAM. Why?

LEN. Yeh.

PAM. Sorry then?

LEN. Tell us.

PAM. 'Ow many girls you 'ad?

LEN. No, I tol' yer my life.

PAM. 'Old on.

LEN. What?

PAM. Yer got a spot.

LEN. Where?

PAM. 'Old still.

LEN. Is it big?

PAM. 'Old still.

LEN. Go easy!

PAM. Got it!

LEN. Ow!

She bursts a spot on his neck.

PAM. Give us yer 'anky.

LEN. Yer got it?

PAM. Yeh.

LEN. Ow! It d'narf 'urt.

He gives her his handkerchief. She dips her hand in the water and dries it on the handkerchief. She gives it back to him.

PAM. Yer wan'a wash sometimes.

LEN. Cheeky cow. (*Slight pause. They are both lying down.*) Yer wouldn't go back with any ol' sod?

PAM. You are rotten.

LEN. I'm sorry. Pam?

PAM. You're 'urtin' me leg.

LEN. I'm sorry.

PAM. No.

LEN. When yer goin' a start me jumper?

PAM (*still annoyed*). Why d'yer 'ave t' say that?

LEN. Tell us about me jumper.

PAM. Ain' got no wool.

LEN. I'll get it t'morra. An' we'll start lookin' for a place t'morra.

PAM. No places round 'ere.

LEN. Move out a bit. It's better out.

PAM. Yer'll be lucky.

LEN. Bin lucky with you. (*His head is in her lap. He twists so that he can put his arms round her.*) Ain' I bin lucky with you?

PAM. Yer don't deserve it.

LEN. I said I'm sorry – I won't arst no more. It's me good looks done it.

PAM. It *was* you. It weren't no one else.

LEN. Less go t'bed early t'night.

PAM. If yer go t' bed much earlier it won't be worth gettin' up.

LEN. Lovely. 'Ow about a sing-song.

PAM. No.

LEN (*sings*).

> Be kind to'yer four-footed friends
> That duck may be somebody's brother
> Yer may think that this is the end
> Well it is.

Slight pause.

They must a' forgot us. We bin 'ere 'ours.

PAM. Do the rest.

LEN. Some mothers!

Pause.

Livin' like that must 'a got yer down.

PAM. Used to it.

LEN. They ought to be shot.

PAM: Why?

LEN. Don't it every worry yer?

PAM. Ow?

LEN. Supposed you turned out like that?

PAM. No.

LEN. 'Ow'd it start?

PAM. Never arst.

LEN. No one said?

PAM. Never listen. It's their life.

LEN. But –

PAM. Yer can't do nothin', yer know. No one'll thank yer.

LEN. 'Ow long's it bin goin' on?

PAM. Longer'n I know.

Pause. He sits and leans towards her.

LEN. Must a' bin bloody rotten when yer was a kid.

PAM. Never know'd no difference. They 'ad a boy in the war.

LEN. Theirs?

PAM. Yeh.

LEN. I ain't seen 'im.

PAM. Dead.

LEN. O.

PAM. A bomb in a park.

LEN. That what made 'em go funny?

PAM. No. I come after.

LEN. What a life.

PAM. I 'ad me moments.

LEN. I won't turn out like that. I wouldn't arst yer if I didn't know better 'n that. That sort of carry-on ain' fair.

PAM. I know.

LEN. We'll get on ail right. I wonder it never sent yer off yer nut.

PAM. Yer don't notice.

LEN. It won't be long now. Why don't yer blow up an' knock their 'eads t'gether?

PAM (*shrugs*). I 'ope I never see 'em again. Thass all.

Slight pause. LEN *looks round.*

LEN. I ain' got a decent jumper.

Pause.

'Ow'd they manage?

PAM. When?

LEN. They writes notes or somethin'?

PAM. No.

LEN. 'Ow's that?

PAM. No need.

LEN. They must.

PAM. No.

LEN. Why?

PAM. Nothin' t' say. 'E puts 'er money over the fire every Friday, an' thass all there is. Talk about somethin' else.

LEN. Whass she say about 'im?

PAM. Nothin'.

LEN. But –

PAM. She never mentions 'im an' 'e never mentions 'er. I don' wanna talk about it.

LEN. They never mention each other?

PAM. I never 'eard 'em.

LEN. Not once?

PAM. *No!*

LEN. It's wet down 'ere.

Pause.

I ain' livin' with me in-laws, thass a fact.

FRED (*off*). Four!

LEN. I never got yer placed till I saw yer ol' people.

PAM. I never chose 'em!

LEN. I never meant that! –

PAM. Don't know why yer wan'a keep on about 'em!

LEN. – I never try an' get at yer!

FRED *comes on down right. His back to the audience.*

FRED. Number-four-bang-on-the-door!

PAM. Thass us.

FRED. Less 'ave yer!

LEN. Less stay out!

PAM. Why?

FRED. Oi!

PAM (*to* LEN). Come on.

LEN. We're a pirate ship.

FRED (*taking the micky*). You devil!

PAM. Yer'll 'ave t' pay.

LEN. Come an' get us!

FRED. Wass up darlin'? 'As 'e got 'is rudder stuck?

PAM (*to* LEN). I'm 'ungry.

LEN. Why didn't yer say?

LEN *starts to pull in.* FRED *moves towards them as the boat comes in.*

FRED. Lovely. 'Elp 'im darlin'. Thass lovely. She 'andles that like a duchess 'andles a navvy's pick.

LEN. All right?

FRED. Lovely.

He leans out and jerks the boat in. PAM *stands awkwardly.*

LEN. Steady.

FRED. 'Old tight, darlin'.

He lifts her out.

Yer wanna watch Captain Blood there. Very nice.

LEN. Okay?

PAM. Ta.

FRED. Very 'ow's yer father.

LEN (*stepping out*). Muddy.

PAM (*to* LEN). I enjoyed that.

FRED. Same 'ere.

LEN. We'll do it again.

FRED. Any time.

PAM (*to* LEN). Got everythin'?

FRED (*to* PAM). You 'ave.

LEN (*clowning*). Watch it!

FRED. 'Oo's bin' 'aving a bash on me duckboards?

PAM (*to* LEN). Less 'ave me bag.

FRED. Bashin's extra.

PAM. Yer wanna get yerself a job.

FRED. I got one.

PAM. 'Irin' out boats!

FRED. I'd rather 'ire you out, darlin'.

LEN (*joking*). Watch it!

PAM (*to* LEN). Ready?

LEN. Yeh.

LEN *and* PAM *start to go right.*

FRED. Why, you got a job for us? I wouldn't mind a bit a
grind for you.

PAM. Yer'll 'ave t' join the union.

FRED. I'm in, love. Paid up.

LEN (*joking*). Yer'll be in the splash in a minute.

LEN *and* PAM *go out left.*

FRED (*to himself*). Right up. Like you, darlin'.

SCENE THREE

Park. Bare stage.

PETE, BARRY, MIKE, COLIN. PETE *wears a brown suit and
suede shoes. The jacket is short in the seat and tight on the
shoulders. His tie is black. The others wear jeans and shirts.*

MIKE. What time they bury the bugger?

PETE. Couldn't tell yer.

COLIN. Don' yer wan'a go?

PETE. Leave off! 'Oo's goin' a make me time up?

COLIN. Why yer goin' then?

PETE. The ol' lady'll ruck if I don't.

MIKE. Yeh, they reckon anythin' like this.

COLIN. Blinkin' morbid.

MIKE. Looks lovely in a black tie don' 'e!

They laugh.

PETE. What a carry on! 'E come runnin' round be'ind the
bus. Only a nipper. Like a flash I thought right yer nasty
bastard. Only ten or twelve. I jumps right down on me
revver an' bang I got 'im on me off-side an' 'e shoots right
out under this lorry comin' straight on.

MIKE. Crunch.

COLIN. Blood all over the shop.

MIKE. The Fall a the Roman Empire.

PETE. This lorry was doin' a ton in a built-up street.

BARRY. Garn! Yer never seen 'im.

PETE. No?

BARRY. 'It 'im before yer knew 'e was comin'.

PETE (*lighting his pipe*). Think I can't drive?

COLIN. What a giggle, though.

MIKE. Accidents is legal.

COLIN. Can't touch yer.

PETE. This coroner-twit says 'e's sorry for troublin' me.

MIKE. The law thanks 'im for 'is 'elp.

PETE. They paid me for comin'.

MIKE. An' the nip's mother reckons 'e ain' got a blame 'isself.

COLIN. She'll turn up at the funeral.

PETE. Rraammmmmmmmmm!

COLIN. Bad for the body work.

MIKE. Can't yer claim insurance?

PETE. No.

MIKE. Choked!

COLIN. Ruined 'is paint work.

BARRY. 'E's 'avin' yer on!

MIKE. Yer creep.

COLIN. Yer big creep.

PETE. Let 'im alone. 'E don't know no better.

COLIN. 'E don't know nothin'.

MIKE. Big stingy creep.

COLIN. Yer wouldn't 'ave the guts.

BARRY. No guts?

MIKE. Yeh.

BARRY. Me?

COLIN. Not yer grannie.

BARRY. I done blokes in.

MIKE. 'Ere we go.

BARRY. More'n you 'ad 'ot dinners. In the jungle. Shootin'
   up the yeller-niggers. An' cut 'em up after with the ol'
   pig-sticker. Yeh.

MIKE (*hoots*).

COLIN. Do leave off!

BARRY. You lot wouldn't know a stiff if it sat up and shook
   'ands with yer!

MIKE. Aa! Shootin' up the yeller-nigs!

COLIN. Sounds like brothers a your'n.

BARRY. Get stuffed!

PETE (*to them all*). Chuck it, eh?

COLIN. Yeller-niggers! My life! What yer scratchin'?

MIKE. 'E's got a dose.

PETE. Ain' surprisin'.

COLIN. Ain' it dropped off yet?

MIKE. Tied on with a ol' johnny.

COLIN. It's 'is girl.

MIKE. 'Is what?

PETE. Gunged-up ol' boot.

COLIN. 'E knocked it off in the back a 'is car last night –
MIKE. 'Is what?
PETE. Pile a ol' scrap.
MIKE. Ought a be put off the road.
COLIN. 'E was knockin' it off in the back an' –
MIKE. I 'eard.
PETE. What?
MIKE. The back-bumper fell off.
PETE. Yeh?
COLIN. I's a fact!
PETE. My life!
MIKE. An' what she say?
COLIN. Yer juss drop somethin'.
BARRY. Bollocks!

He laughs at himself.

MIKE. Yeh!
COLIN. 'Aving trouble with yer 'orn?
BARRY. It weren't no bumper! Me fog lamp come off.
MIKE. 'Is fog lamp!

They roar with laughter.

COLIN. I knew somethin' come off!
MIKE. Flippin' fog lamp!
PETE. Thass what she calls it!
COLIN. Wonder it weren't 'is engine come out.
BARRY. Better'n nothin'.
MIKE. Yer couldn't knock someone down with that!
PETE. It'd come t' a stop.
MIKE. Shootin' up the yeller-niggers!
BARRY. Yeh, yer ain' lived!

LEN *comes on down right.*

PETE. Me mum's got a dirty great wreath.
MIKE. Yeh!

COLIN. Give somethin' for it?

PETE. I ain' a 'ippocrit.

COLIN. Oi – whass-yer-name!

LEN. Eh?

COLIN. It's – Lenny, ain' it?

LEN. Yeh. – O! 'Ow's it goin', admiral?

COLIN. 'Ow's yerself?

LEN. Not so dodgy. Long time.

COLIN. Me and 'im was t'school t'gether.

MIKE. Yeh?

COLIN. What yer bin doin'?

BARRY. Reform school?

MIKE. Don't 'e show yer up!

COLIN. Take no notice. Creep! – Workin'?

LEN. Worse luck.

COLIN. I couldn't place yer for a minute. (*Slight pause.*) Yeh.

LEN. Yer ain' changed much.

BARRY. What yer doin' now?

LEN. Waitin'.

MIKE. I – I!

COLIN. It was in the park, yer 'onour!

MIKE. This girl come up t'me.

COLIN. An' drags me in the bushes.

BARRY. Yer 'onour.

He laughs.

COLIN. I knew she was thirteen.

MIKE. But she twisted me arm.

COLIN. An' 'er ol' dad 'd bin bashin' it off for years.

BARRY. Yer 'onour.

He laughs.

COLIN. Twisted yer what?

MIKE. Never know yer luck!

COLIN. Married?

LEN. Gettin' ready.
BARRY. 'Oo with?
LEN. We're waitin' –
COLIN. Pull the other one!
MIKE. What for?
PETE. Till she drops 'er nipper.
COLIN. Else it looks bad goin' up the aisle.
MIKE. She can 'ide it be'ind 'er flowers.
BARRY. Is that what they carry 'em for?
COLIN. We live an' learn.
MIKE. Takes all sorts.

MARY *comes on up right.*

LEN. Thass us.
COLIN. *That?*

LEN *goes to* MARY.

PETE. One man's meat.
MIKE. More like scrag-end.
BARRY. Bit past it, ain' she?
PETE. She's still got the regulation 'oles.
MIKE. Experience 'elps. Yer get a surprise sometimes.
LEN (*to* MARY). Less give yer a 'and.
MARY. Whew! Ta.

She gives him the shopping bags.

LEN. Okay?
MARY. I was juss goin' ter drop 'em.
MIKE. 'Ear that.
BARRY. Goin' a drop 'em!
COLIN. In the park?
MIKE. At 'alf-past twelve?
PETE (*laughing*). The dirty ol' scrubber.

LEN *and* MARY *start to cross left.*

BARRY (*to* COLIN). That what they taught yer at school?

COLIN *whistles.*

LEN (*amused*). Put a sock in it.

BARRY. What yer got at the top a your legs? What time 's breakfast?

MARY. That your mates?

LEN. They're juss 'avin' a laugh.

MARY. You all right with them bags?

LEN. Yeh.

COLIN. Roger the lodger 'ad a bad cough.

MIKE. 'E sneezed so 'ard.

COLIN. 'Is door knob fell off.

BARRY. 'Is landlady said we'll soon 'ave yer well.

COLIN. So she pulled off 'er drawers.

MIKE. An' polished 'is bell!

MARY. Lot a roughs.

LEN *and* MARY *go out left.*

PETE. Makes yer think.

COLIN. What?

PETE. Never know what yer missin'.

MIKE. True.

PETE. I knew a bloke once reckoned 'e knocked off 'is grannie.

COLIN. Yeh?

PETE. All a mistake.

COLIN. 'Ow's that?

PETE. There was a power cut at the time an' –

BARRY. – 'E thought it was 'is sister.

PETE. Ain' yer clever!

MIKE. Trust the unions!

COLIN. Makes yer think, though.

BARRY *blows a raspberry.*

PETE (*smoking his pipe*). Never know 'alf what goes on.

MIKE. That age she must be 'angin' out for it.

PETE. Stuffin' it all in before it's too late.

COLIN. Yeh.

There is a slight pause.

PETE. Ooorrr! I'll 'ave t' fix up a little bird t'night. 'Ere, wass
the time?

COLIN. Time we're back t' work.

They groan.

MIKE (*to* PETE). Time yer're round the church they'll 'ave
'im down the 'ole or up the chimney or wherever 'e's goin'.

PETE. I reckon they wanna put 'im down the 'ole an' p'
the chain.

SCENE FOUR

The living room. Dark.

The door opens. MARY *comes in. She puts on the light.* HARRY
is sitting in the armchair. He is partly asleep. MARY *puts sauce,
salt and pepper on the table and goes out.* HARRY *gets up. He goes
to the door and puts the light out. He goes back to the armchair.*
Pause.

The door opens. MARY *comes in. She puts on the light. She
takes knife, fork, spoon and table napkin to the table. She lays the
napkin as a small table cloth. The door opens.* PAM *comes in.
She wears a slip and carries a hair brush and cosmetics. She
switches on the TV set.* MARY *goes out. Without waiting to
adjust the set* PAM *goes to the couch and sits. She makes up her
face. The door opens.* MARY *comes in with a plate of food.*

MARY (*calls*). It's on the table.

She walks towards the table. To PAM.

I told you not to walk round like that.

MARY *puts the food on the table and goes out.* PAM *goes to the TV set and adjusts it. She goes back to the couch and sits. She makes up her face.* MARY *comes in.*

(*At the door*). It's on the table! That's the second time!

She goes to the TV set.

I don't know 'ow they 'ave the nerve to put it on.

She switches to another channel. She steps back to look at the picture. She steps forward to adjust it. She steps back.

Hm.

She steps forward and adjusts it again.

If yer put it in the oven it goes 'ard as nails.

She steps back and looks at the set. She goes to the couch, sits and watches TV. Pause.

PAM. More like one a them daft mirrors at a circus.
MARY. The man'll 'ave to come an' fix it.

She goes to the set and adjusts it.

You don't know 'ow to switch it on. It goes all right when I do it.

LEN *comes in.*

LEN. Smells great.
MARY. You've let it ruin.
LEN. Nah.
MARY. Cold as Christmas.
LEN. Do me.

He sits at the table and eats.

MARY (*goes to the set and re-adjusts it*). I don't know. – Did yer put the light out in the scullery?
LEN. Yeh.

MARY. We need a new one. That's what's wrong with it.

She goes back to the couch and sits. She watches silently. Pause.

PAM. Looks like one a them black an' white minstrels.
MARY. Well you do it, an' don't sit there pokin' 'oles.
PAM. I ain' watchin'.
MARY. Sounds like it.

LEN *eats.* MARY *watches.* PAM *makes up.* HARRY *is still.
The TV is fairly loud. A very long pause.*
   *Slowly a baby starts to cry. It goes on crying without a break
until the end of the scene. Nothing happens until it has cried a
long while. Then* MARY *speaks.*

   Can yer see?
LEN. Yeh.
MARY. Move yer seat.
LEN. I can see.

Pause.

   Yer a fair ol' cook.
MARY. It's ruined. Yer get no encouragement t' try.

Pause. The baby screams with rage. After a while MARY *lifts
her head in the direction of the screams.*

   Pam-laa!

Slight pause. PAM *stands and puts her cosmetics in a little bag.
She goes to the TV set. She turns up the volume. She goes back
to the couch and sits.*

   There's plenty of left-overs.
LEN. Full up.
MARY. An' there's rhubarb and custard.
LEN: O.

Pause. The baby chokes.

PAM. Too lazy t' get up an' fetch it.

MARY. Don't start. Let's 'ave a bit a peace for one night.

Pause.

PAM. 'Is last servant died a over-work.

LEN. I ain' finished this, nosey.

MARY. Why don't yer shut that kid up.

PAM. I can't.

MARY. Yer don't try.

PAM. Juss cries louder when I go near it.

MARY (*watching TV*). I ain' goin' up for yer. (*Still watching TV.*) High time it 'ad a father. (*To* LEN). There's plenty a tea in the pot.

LEN (*watching TV*). Yeh.

MARY (*watching TV*). That's what it needs. No wonder it cries. (*Pause. To* LEN.) Busy?

LEN. Murder.

MARY (*watching TV*). Weather don't 'elp.

LEN (*still watching TV*). Eh? (*The baby whimpers pitifully. Pause. Still watching TV.*) Ha!

Pause. PAM *picks up her things and goes out.*

MARY. About time.

LEN. Wan'a cup?

MARY. No. There's milk in that custard. It'll only get thrown out.

LEN (*stands*). I'll bust.

He goes out.

MARY (*calls*). On the top shelf.

LEN (*off*). What?

MARY. It's on the top shelf!

Pause. LEN *comes in. He carries a plate to the table.*

Did yer get it?

LEN. Yeh.

He sits.

MARY. Shut that door, Len. Me 'ead's playin' me up again.
LEN. Take some a yer anadins.
MARY. I've 'ad too many t'day. Thass what makes it worse.

LEN *goes back to the door and shuts it. He goes to the table and eats.*

Did yer put the oven out?
LEN. An' the light.
MARY. I ain' made a money, y'know.

Suddenly the baby cries much louder.

Put some sugar on it.

LEN *sprinkles the sugar from a teaspoon.*

People'll send the police round 'ere next.
LEN. It'll cry itself t'sleep.

PAM *comes in. She wears a dress.*

MARY. It's still cryin'.
PAM. I thought the cat was stuck up the chimney.

She sits on the couch and pulls up her stockings.

'Ad a good look? – I'm tired a 'im watchin' me all the time.
MARY. I told yer t' get dressed in the scullery like anybody else.
PAM. I can dress where I like in me own 'ome.
LEN (*to himself*). O no.
PAM. You say somethin'?
LEN (*calmly*). Yeh – shut up.
PAM. I suppose that's your idea a good manners.

Pause.

When yer leavin' us? I'm sick an' tired a arstin'.

MARY. I don't wanna 'ear all this again t'night.

PAM. 'E gets on me nerves.

LEN. I ain' leavin' that kid.

PAM. Why?

LEN. With you?

PAM. It ain' your kid.

LEN. No?

PAM. Yer'll 'ave t' take my word for it.

LEN. Yer don't even know when you're lyin'.

Pause. The baby cries.

PAM. I don't understan' yer. Yer ain' got no self respect.

LEN. You 'ave like.

PAM. No one with any self respect wouldn't wanna stay.

LEN *pours tea for himself.*

Yer'll 'ave t'go sometime. Yer can't juss 'ang on till yer rot.

MARY. Pack it up! No wonder that kid cries!

PAM. Why don't you tell 'im t' go? It's your job. 'E's gettin' on me nerves every night. If it goes on much longer I'll be ill.

MARY. That'll teach yer t'bring fellas back.

PAM (*to* HARRY). Why don't you tell im? It's your 'ouse. There's bin nothin' but rows an' arguments ever since 'e got 'ere. I've 'ad all I can stand! (*Slight pause.*) Dad!

HARRY. I ain' gettin' involved. Bound t'be wrong.

PAM (*to* LEN). I don't understan' yer. Yer can't enjoy stayin' 'ere.

LEN *drinks his tea.*

It's bad enough bein' stuck with a kid without 'avin' you 'anging roun' me neck. The 'ole street's laughin' be'ind yer back.

LEN. I ain' leavin' that kid.

PAM. Take it.

LEN. With me?

PAM. 'Ow else?

MARY. 'Ow can 'e?

PAM. Thass 'is worry.

MARY. 'E can't look after a kid.

PAM. Put it on the council.

MARY (*shrugs*). They wouldn't 'ave it if they've got any sense.

The baby cries.

PAM. Well?

LEN. Kids need proper 'omes.

PAM. Yer see!

LEN (*looks in the teapot*). Out a' water.

He goes out.

MARY. Wouldn't yer miss it?

PAM. That racket?

The baby whimpers. There is a ring. PAM *goes out.* MARY *quickly tidies the couch.* LEN *comes back with the teapot.*

MARY. Did the door go?

LEN (*nods*). Juss then.

FRED (*off*). All right, all right. I said I'm sorry, ain' I?

PAM *is heard indistinctly.*

    Well let's say 'allo first!

FRED *comes in.*

    'Evenin'. 'Evenin', ma.

MARY. We're just watchin' telly.

FRED. Anythin' interestin'?

MARY. Come in.

FRED. 'Lo, Len. 'Ow's life?

LEN. Usual. 'Ow's the job?

FRED. Don't talk about it.

PAM *comes in*.

PAM. I still don't see 'ow that makes yer all

FRED. Give it a rest, Pam.

PAM. The same last time.

MARY. Take yer coat off.

PAM. Yer oughta let me know if yer're goin'a be late.

FRED. 'Ow could I? Sorry love. We'll juss 'ave t' make it later in future.

PAM (*to* MARY). Can I put the kid in your room?

MARY. No wonder it can't sleep. Pushed around like some ol' door mat.

PAM. Can I or can't I? I ain' sittin' there with that row goin' on.

MARY. Do what yer like.

FRED (*to* PAM). Got plenty a fags?

MARY. Yer will anyway.

PAM (*to* FRED). Ready?

FRED. See yer, Lenny boy.

LEN. Yeh.

PAM. It's all the same if I was meetin' yer outside in the street. I'd be left standin' in the cold.

FRED (*following* PAM *to the door*). Got any fags? I left mine be'ind.

PAM *and* FRED *go out*. LEN *stacks the things on the table and takes some of them out. The baby's crying suddenly gets louder.* LEN *comes in again. He picks up the sauce and the table napkin and goes out.* MARY *turns off the TV set and goes out.* HARRY *goes to the table and pours himself tea.* LEN *comes back.*

LEN. O.

HARRY. Finished.

LEN. Ta.

Pause.

..sh t'God I could take that kid out a this.

ARRY (*drinks*). Better.

LEN. No life growin' up 'ere.

HARRY (*wipes his mouth on the back of his hand*). Ah.

LEN. Wish t' God I 'ad some place.

HARRY. Yer wan'a keep yer door shut.

LEN. What?

HARRY. T'night.

LEN. Me door?

HARRY. Yer always keep yer door open when 'e's sleepin' with 'er.

LEN. I listen out for the kid. They ain' bothered.

MARY (*off*). Night, Len.

LEN (*calls*). Night. (*To* HARRY.) More?

HARRY. No.

LEN. Plenty in the pot.

HARRY (*wipes his mouth on the back of his hand*). Yer'll catch cold with it open.

LEN (*holding the teapot*). Night, then.

He goes to the door.

HARRY (*sitting in the armchair*). Put that light out.

LEN *puts the light out and goes. The crying sobs away to silence.*

SCENE FIVE

LEN's *bedroom. It is shaped like the living-room. Furniture: a single bed up right, a wooden chair close to it.* PAM *is in bed.* LEN *stands centre, away from her.*

LEN. Did yer take yer medicine?

Pause.

Feelin' better?

PAM. I'm movin' down t' me own room t'morra. Yer'll 'ave t' move back up 'ere.

LEN. Quieter up 'ere.

PAM. Like a blinkin' grave.

LEN. Why don't yer 'ave the telly up?

PAM. No.

LEN. Easy fix a plug.

PAM. Did yer see Fred?

LEN. Yer never took yer medicine. (*He pours her medicine and gives it to her.*) 'Ere. (PAM *takes it.*) Say ta. (*She drinks it and gives a small genuine* 'Ugh!') Read yer magazines?

PAM. Did Fred say anythin'?

MARY (*off*). Pam-laa! She gettin' up, Len?

PAM (*to herself*). O God.

MARY (*off*). The doctor says there's nothin' t' stop yer gettin' up. Yer're as well as I am.

LEN *closes the door but the voice is still heard.*

Pam-laa! The dinner's on the table.

LEN. Yer better off up 'ere out a 'er way.

PAM. The cow.

LEN *straightens the bed.*

Leave that.

LEN. You're comin' undone.

PAM. Leave it.

LEN. It's all –

PAM. I said leave it!

LEN (*continuing*). Someone's got a give yer a 'and.

PAM. I won't 'ave yer pullin' me about.

LEN (*walking away*). Why don't yer sit in a chair for 'alf 'our?

PAM. Mind yer own business.

LEN. Yer ain't doin' yerself no good lyin' there.

MARY (*off*). She gettin' up?

LEN. I'm only tryin' a 'elp.

PAM. Don't want yer 'elp.

LEN. Yer got bugger all idea 'ow to look after yerself.

PAM. Go away.

LEN. Some one –

PAM. For Ch-issake!

LEN. Someone's got a stick up for yer. (*Slight pause.*) Yer treated me like dirt. But I ain't goin' a carry on like that.

MARY (*off*). Pamm-laa!

PAM (*calls*). Shut up! I'm sick a' the lot of yer! (*Slight pause.*) Shut up!

LEN *goes out.*

PAM. Thank Chriss for that.

MARY (*off*). She up yet?

LEN *answers indistinctly. Pause.* PAM *pulls out the blankets that* LEN *tucked in.* LEN *comes back with the baby.*

LEN (*to baby*). 'Ello then! 'Ello then!

PAM. O no.

LEN. Look-ee that. 'Oo that mummy-there?

PAM. She's got the grub out on the table.

LEN. It'll keep.

PAM. She ain' better row me out for it.

LEN. Take it.

PAM. Put it back.

LEN. Yer ought a take it.

PAM. Don't keep tellin' me what I ought a do.

LEN. Yer ain' even looked at it for weeks.

PAM. Ain' going to.

LEN. Yer'd feel better.

Pause.

'Ello then.

PAM. Did yer give 'im what I wrote?

LEN. 'E's busy, 'e reckons. It's 'is busy time.

PAM. Ha!

LEN. 'Avin' yourn on a tray?

PAM. If yer like.

LEN. It knows yer voice.

PAM. Put it away before it starts.

LEN. Good for its lungs.

PAM. Yer d'narf annoy me, Len.

LEN. I know.

PAM. Yer're always pesterin' me.

LEN. Someone's got a look after yer.

PAM. There yer are! Thass another annoyin' thing t' say. (*She sits.*) This dump gives me the 'ump. Put that away.

LEN. Yer can't let it lie on its back all day. Someone's got a pick it up.

PAM (*sitting back*). Why should I worry? Its father don't give a damn. I could be dyin' an' 'e can't find ten minutes.

LEN. I'm blowed if I'm goin' a put meself out if yer can't co-operate.

He tries to put the baby in her arms.

PAM. I tol' yer take it back! Get off a me! Yer bloody lunatic! Bleedin' cheek! (*Calls.*) Mum!

LEN. You 'ave it for a change!

He puts the baby on the bed.

PAM. Yer goin' mad! It's fallin'. Catch it!

LEN *puts the baby so that it is safe.*

LEN. I ain' your paid nurse!

PAM (*calls*). Mum! – I know why Fred ain' come – yer bin tearin' up me letters.

LEN. 'E did!

PAM. Yer little liar! (*She turns away from the baby.*) I ain' touchin' it.

LEN. It'll stay there all night!

PAM. Thass what yer call 'elpin' me.

Pause. LEN *picks up the baby.*

See!

LEN. Can't give it a cold juss because we're rowin'.

He goes towards the door. He stops.

'E said 'e'd look in.

PAM (*she turns round*). When? (*She turns back to the wall.*) What did 'e say?

LEN. I said yer wanted to see 'im. 'E goes 'e's up to 'is eyes in it. So I said I got a couple of tickets for Crystal Palace. 'E's knockin' off early.

PAM. Saturday?

LEN. T'night.

PAM (*turns*). Yer got 'im downstairs!

LEN. No.

PAM (*calls*). Mum – is Fred there? Fred? – 'E might be early.

LEN. There's a good 'alf 'our yet.

PAM (*excited*). I 'ope 'is lot wins.

LEN. 'E might be late.

PAM. Not for football. Yer can say she's upstairs if yer wan' a go. Put it like that.

LEN (*looks at child*). 'E's well away.

PAM. I ain' cut me nails all the time I bin in bed.

MARY (*off*). Lennie!

LEN. Shall I get the scissors?

PAM. She won't shut up till yer go down. I got me own.

MARY (*off*). Leonard! I keep callin' yer. (*Outside the door.*) 'Ow many more times. (*She comes in.*) I bin callin' the last 'alf 'our. Dinner won't be fit t'eat.

LEN. Juss puttin' the nipper back.

MARY. That's the last time I cook a 'ot meal in this 'ouse. I mean it this time. (*To* PAM.) Yer can make yer own bed

t'morra, you. (*To* LEN.) I ain' sweatin' over a 'ot stove.
No one offers t'buy me a new one. (*To* PAM.) I can't afford
t' keep yer on yer national 'ealth no longer. I'm the one 'oo
ought to be in bed.

MARY *goes out.*

PAM. I got all patches under me eyes.
LEN. No.
PAM. I feel awful.
LEN. Yer look nice.
PAM. I'll 'ave t' 'ave a wash.
LEN. Yeh.

SCENE SIX

The Park. A bare stage. FRED *holds a fishing-rod out over the
stalls. He wears jeans and an old dull leather jacket.* LEN *sits
beside him on a small tin box. On the ground there are a bait
box, odds and ends box, float box, milk bottle, sugar bottle, flask
and net.*

LEN. Round our place t'night?
FRED. No.
LEN. It's Saturday.
FRED. O yeh.
LEN. She won't like it.
FRED. No.

Pause.

   Yer wan' a get yerself a good rod.
LEN. Can't afford it.

FRED. Suit yerself.

LEN. Lend us yourn.

FRED. Get knotted.

Slight pause.

LEN. I in yer way then?

FRED. Eh?

LEN. Sittin' 'ere.

FRED. Free country.

LEN. Yer'd never think it.

FRED. Nippy.

LEN. Lend us yer jacket.

FRED. Jump in.

LEN. 'Ow much yer give for that?

FRED. Yer get 'em on h.p.

LEN. Fair bit a work.

FRED (*runs his hand along the rod*). Comes in 'andy.

Pause.

LEN. She said yer was comin' round for the telly.

FRED. News t' me.

LEN. Don't know whass on.

FRED. Don't care.

LEN. Never looked. (*Slight pause.*) Never bothers me. Easy find out from the paper if yer –

FRED. Don't keep on about it.

LEN. Eh?

FRED. Don't bloody well keep on about it.

LEN. Suits me. (*Slight pause.*) I was agreein' with yer. I thought like –

FRED. Oi – Len, I come out for the fishin'. I don't wanna 'ear all your ol' crap.

Slight pause. LEN *turns his head right and stares at the river.*

'Onest, Len – yer d'narf go on.

LEN. I only said I was agreein' with yer. Blimey, if yer can't ...

He stops. Pause.

FRED. Sod!
LEN. Whass up?
FRED. Bait's gone.
LEN. Gone? They've 'ad it away.
FRED. Never.
LEN. Must 'ave.
FRED. More like wriggled off.
LEN. I mounted it 'ow yer said.
FRED (*winds in*). Come 'ere. Look.

He takes a worm from the worm box.

Right, yer take yer worm. Yer roll it in yer 'and t' knock it out. Thass first. Then yer break a bit off. Cop 'old o' that.

He gives part of the worm to LEN.

LEN. Ta.
FRED. Now yer thread yer 'ook through this bit. Push it up on yer gut. Leave it. – Give us that bit. Ta. Yer thread yer other bit on the 'ook, but yer leave a fair bit 'angin' off like that, why, t'wriggle in the water. Then yer push yer top bit down off the gut and camer-flarge yer shank. Got it?
LEN. Thass 'ow I done it.
FRED. Yeh. Main thing, keep it neat.

He casts. The line hums.

Lovely.

A long silence.

The life.

Silence.

LEN. Down the labour Monday.

FRED *grunts*.

Start somethin'.

Silence.

No life, broke.

FRED. True.

Silence. LEN *pokes in the worm box with a stick.*

Feed 'em on milk.

LEN. Fact?

Silence.

I'll tell 'er yer ain' comin'.

FRED. Len!

LEN. Well yer got a let 'er know.

FRED. 'Oo says?

LEN. Yer can't juss –

FRED. Well?

LEN. Shut up a minute.

FRED. Listen, mate, shut yer trap an' give us a snout.

LEN. No.

FRED. Yer're loaded.

LEN. Scroungin' git! Smoke yer own. – She'll be up 'alf the night. That'll be great. – I reckon yer got a bloody nerve takin' my fags, yer know I'm broke. – Yer believe in keepin' em waitin' for it.

Slight pause.

FRED. Yer used to knock 'er off, that right?

LEN. Once.

FRED. There yer are then.

LEN. What?

FRED. It's all yourn.

LEN. She don't wan'a know.

FRED. 'Ow's that?

LEN. Since you 'ad 'er.

FRED. What d'yer expect? No – they're like that. Once they go off, they go right off.

LEN. Don't even get a feel.

FRED. 'Appens all the time. Give us a snout.

LEN. No.

FRED. Tight arse.

Slight pause.

LEN. Skip?

FRED. Yeh?

LEN. What yer reckon on 'er?

FRED. For a lay?

LEN. Yeh.

FRED. Fair. Depends on the bloke.

LEN. Well?

FRED. No – get that any time.

Silence.

LEN. Gettin' dark.

Silence.

FRED. Call it a day.

LEN. In a minute.

FRED. Never know why yer stick that dump.

LEN. Seen worse.

FRED. I ain'.

Slight pause.

LEN. Skip?

FRED. Whass up now?

LEN. Why's she go for you?

FRED. They all do mate.

LEN. No, why's she – ill over it?

FRED. Come off it, she 'ad a drop a the ol' flu.

LEN. Yeh. But why's she like that?

FRED. It ain' me money.

LEN. They all want the same thing, I reckon. So you must 'ave more a it.

FRED. Thass true! Oi!

LEN. What?

FRED. Still.

Pause.

Thought I 'ad a touch.

Pause.

Nah.

They ease off. FRED looks up at the sky.

Jack it in.

LEN. Anyway, thass what they reckon.

FRED. Eh?

LEN. They all want the same thing.

FRED. O.

LEN. I reckon yer're 'avin' me on.

FRED. Me?

LEN. Like the fish that got away.

FRED. I ain' with yer.

He shakes his head.

LEN. That big! (*He holds his hands eighteen inches apart.*)

FRED (*laughs*). More like that! (*He holds his hands three feet apart.*)

LEN. Ha! Thass why she's sick.

FRED. Now give us a fag.

LEN. No.

FRED (*spits*). 'Ave t' light one a me own.

*He takes one of his own cigarettes from a packet in his breast
pocket. He does not take the packet from the pocket.*

LEN. Mind the moths.

FRED. Yer ever 'ad worms up yer nose, in yer ears, an' down
yer throat?

LEN. Not lately.

FRED. Yer will in a minute.

LEN. Well give us a snout then.

FRED. Slimey ponce!

He gives LEN *a cigarette.* LEN *gives* FRED *a light.*

LEN. I used a 'ear, know that?

FRED. 'Ear what? – 'E's like a flippin' riddle.

LEN. You an' 'er.

FRED. Me an' 'oo?

LEN. On the bash.

FRED. Do what?

LEN. Straight up.

FRED. Chriss.

LEN. Yeh.

FRED. Yer kiddin'.

LEN. On my life. Kep me up 'alf the night. Yer must a bin
trying for the cup.

FRED (*draws his cigarette*). Why didn't yer let on?

LEN. No, it's all a giggle, ain't it?

FRED (*shrugs*). Yeh? Makes yer feel a right charlie.

He drops his cigarette on the floor and treads on it.

Chriss. Thass one good reason for jackin' 'er in.

LEN. Don't start blamin' me.

FRED. An' you was listenin'?

LEN. Couldn't 'elp it.

FRED. O.

He lays his rod on the ground and crouches to pack his things.

Yer didn't mind me goin' round 'er's.

LEN. Same if I did.

FRED. I didn't know like.

LEN. Yer never ruddy thought. Any'ow, I don't mind.

FRED. I thought she was goin' spare.

LEN. Wan'a 'and?

FRED. No. Give us that tin.

He packs in silence.

I reckon it was up t' you t' say. Yer got a tongue in yer
'ead.

Silence. MIKE *comes in. He has a haversack slung from one
shoulder and carries a rod. He wears a small, flashy hat.*

FRED. No luck?

MIKE. Wouldn't feed a cat.

LEN. Waste a time.

MIKE. Same 'ere.

FRED. Got a breeze up.

MIKE. What yer doin'?

FRED. Now?

MIKE. Yeh, t'night.

FRED. Reckon anythin'?

MIKE. Bit a fun.

FRED. Suits me.

MIKE. You're on.

FRED. Up the other end?

MIKE. 'Ow's the cash?

FRED. Broke. You?

MIKE. I'll touch up the ol' lady.

FRED. Get a couple for me.

LEN. That'll pay the fares.

MIKE. Pick yer up roun' your place.

FRED. Not too early. 'Ave a bath first.

MIKE. Never know 'oo yer'll be sleepin' with.

FRED. After eight.

MIKE. I feel juss right for it.

LEN. What?

MIKE. Out on the 'unt.

FRED (*imitates a bullet*). Tschewwwwww!

MIKE. 'E picks 'em up at a 'undred yards.

FRED. It's me magnetic cobblers.

PAM *comes in. She pushes the pram. The hood is up. A long blue sausage balloon floats from a corner of the hood.*

PAM. 'Ello.

FRED. Whass up?

PAM. Out for a walk.

MIKE (*nods at pram*). Bit late for that, ain' it?

PAM (*to* FRED). What yer got?

FRED. Nothin'.

PAM (*tries to look*). Less 'ave a look.

FRED. Nothin' for you!

PAM. Keep yer shirt on.

MIKE. Yer nearly missed us.

PAM (*to* FRED). Don't get so 'airy-ated.

MIKE. We was juss off.

FRED. What yer cartin' that about for?

PAM. Felt like a walk.

FRED. Bit late.

PAM. Why?

FRED. That ought a be in bed.

PAM. Fresh air won't kill it.

FRED. Should a done it earlier.

PAM. Never 'ad time. Why didn't you?

FRED. You know best.

PAM. When yer comin' round?

FRED. I'll look in.

PAM. When?

FRED. I don't know.

PAM. When about?

FRED. Later on.

PAM. Shall I get somethin' to eat?

FRED. No.

PAM. No bother.

FRED. The ol' lady'll 'ave it all set up.

PAM. I got two nice chops.

FRED. Shame.

PAM. Well see 'ow yer feel. There's no one in now. I got rid a 'em.

FRED. Pity yer didn't say.

PAM. What time then?

FRED. I'll be there.

PAM. Sure?

FRED. Yeh.

PAM. Say so if yer ain'.

FRED. I'll be there.

PAM. That means yer won't.

FRED. Up t'you.

PAM. Why don't yer say so?

FRED (picks up his gear. To MIKE). Thass the lot.

PAM. It ain' no fun waitin' in all night for nothin'.

MIKE. Ready?

FRED (takes a look round). Yeh.

PAM. Why can't yer tell the truth for once?

FRED. Fair enough. I ain' comin'.

LEN. Pam –

PAM. Yer 'ad no intention a comin'.

LEN. Yer left the brake off again.

MIKE (to FRED). Okay?

PAM (to LEN). Put it on, clever.

FRED (to MIKE). Yeh.

PAM (to FRED). I knew all along.

FRED. Come on, Pam. Go 'ome.

PAM. Fred.

FRED. I know.

PAM. I didn't mean t' go off. I was goin' a be nice, I still ain' better.

FRED. Go 'ome an' get in the warm. It's late.

LEN (*putting on the brake*). Yer wan' a be more careful.

PAM (*to* FRED). It's my fault. I never stop t'think.

FRED. Yer wan' a stop thinkin' about yerself, I know that.

PAM. It's them pills they give me.

MIKE (*to* FRED). You comin' or ain' yer.

FRED. Yeh.

PAM. No.

FRED. I'll come round one night next week.

PAM. No.

FRED. Monday night. Ow's that?

PAM. Yer'll change yer mind.

FRED. Straight from work.

PAM. Yer said that before.

FRED. It's the best I can offer.

PAM. I can't go back there now.

FRED. Yer'll be okay.

PAM. If I sit on me own in that room another night I'll go round the bend.

FRED. Yer got the kid.

PAM. Juss t'night. I couldn't stand it on me own no more. I 'ad a come out. I don't know what I'm doin'. That kid ought a be in bed. Less take it 'ome, Fred. It's 'ad new-moanier once.

FRED. You take it 'ome.

PAM. Juss this last time? I won't arst no more. I'll get mum t' stay in with me.

FRED. It's no use.

PAM. Yer ain' seen it in a long time, 'ave yer?

She turns the pram round.

It's puttin' on weight.

FRED. Eh?

PAM. It don't cry like it used to. Not all the time.

MIKE. Past carin'.

PAM. Doo-dee-doo-dee. Say da-daa.

FRED. Yeh, lovely.

He looks away.

LEN (*looking at the baby*). Blind.

PAM (*to* LEN). Like a top.

FRED. What yer give it?

PAM. Asprins.

FRED. That all right?

PAM. Won't wake up till t'morra. It won't disturb yer. What time'll I see yer?

FRED. I'll look in. I ain' sayin' definite.

PAM. I don't mind. Long as I know yer're comin'.

FRED. All right.

PAM. Pity t' waste the chops. I think I'll do 'em in case –

FRED. Yeh, right. It's all accordin'.

PAM. I'll wait up.

FRED. It'll be late, see.

PAM. Thass all right.

FRED. Pam.

PAM. I'll treat meself t' box a choclits.

FRED. There's plenty a blokes knockin' about. Why don't yer pick on someone else.

PAM. No.

MIKE. Yer can 'ave me, darlin'. But yer'll 'ave t' learn a bit more respect.

PAM. 'Ow can I get out with that 'angin' round me neck? 'Oo's goin' a look at me?

FRED. Yer ol' girl'll take it off yer 'ands.

MIKE. Drop 'er a few bob.

FRED. Yer don't try.

PAM. I can't!

FRED. Yer'll 'ave to.

PAM. I can't! I ain' goin' to!

FRED. I ain' goin' a see yer no more.

PAM. No.

FRED. We got a sort this out some time.

PAM. Yer promised!

FRED. It's a waste a time!

PAM. *They* 'eard!

FRED. No.

MIKE. Come on, mate.

FRED. It's finished.

MIKE. Thank Chriss. Less shift!

PAM. Juss t'night. I don't care if yer bin with yer girls. Come 'ome after. Juss once. I won't bother yer. I'll let yer sleep. Please.

FRED. Chriss.

PAM. O what d'you care? I was flat on me back three bloody weeks! 'Oo lifted a finger? I could a bin dyin'! No one!

She starts pushing the pram.

MIKE. Good riddance!

PAM (*stops*). You're that kid's father! Yeh! Yer ain't wrigglin' out a that!

FRED. Prove it.

PAM. I *know*!

FRED. You *know*?

MIKE. Chriss.

FRED. 'Alf the bloody manor's bin through you.

PAM. Rotten liar!

FRED. Yeh?

  To MIKE. Ain' you 'ad 'er?

MIKE. Not yet.

FRED. Yer'll be next.

Points to LEN.

  What about 'im?

To LEN. Eh?

To MIKE. Your's must be the only stiff outside the church-yard she ain' knocked off.

PAM. I 'ate you!

FRED. Now we're gettin' somewhere.

PAM. Pig!

FRED. Thass better. Now piss off!

PAM. I will.

MIKE. Ta-ta!

PAM. An' yer can take yer bloody bastard round yer tart's!
Tell 'er it's a present from me!

PAM *goes out. She leaves the pram.*

MIKE. Lovely start t' the evenin's entertainment.

FRED (*calls*). I ain' takin' it! It'll bloody stay 'ere!

MIKE. What yer wan'a let 'er get away with –

FRED. Don't you start! I 'ad enough with 'er!

LEN. I'd better go after 'er.

FRED. Send 'er back.

LEN. See 'ow she is.

LEN *goes out after* PAM.

FRED (*calls*). Don't leave 'er kid. Take it with yer.

MIKE *whistles after her.* FRED *throws his gear down.*
Lumbered!

MIKE. 'E'll send 'er back.

FRED. 'E ain' got the gumption. We'll drop it in on the way back.

MIKE. Leave it 'ere. Won't be worth goin' time we're ready.

FRED. Give it five minutes.

MIKE. Yer won't see 'er again.

FRED. That won't be the worst thing in me life.

MIKE. Can't yer arst your Liz t' look after it?

FRED. She'd tear me eyes out.

Pause. They sit.

MIKE. They opened that new church on the corner.

FRED. What?

MIKE. They got a club.

FRED. O yeh.

MIKE. We'll 'ave a quick little case round.

FRED. T'night?

MIKE. Yeh.

FRED. Get stuffed.

MIKE. Straight up.

FRED. Pull the other one.

MIKE. Best place out for'n easy pick up.

FRED. Since when?

MIKE. I done it before. There's little pieces all over the shop, nothin' a do.

FRED. Fact?

MIKE. The ol' bleeder shuts 'is eyes for prayers an' they're touchin' 'em up all over the place. Then the law raided this one an' they 'ad it shut down.

FRED. Do leave off.

PETE *and* COLIN *come in right.*

PETE. 'Ow's it then?

MIKE. Buggered up.

COLIN. Like your arse.

MIKE. Like your flippin' ear in a minute.

PETE. I – I!

COLIN. Wass on t'night?

MIKE. Laugh.

BARRY *comes in after* PETE *and* COLIN.

BARRY. Fishin'?

FRED. 'Angin' the Chrissmas decorations.

BARRY. 'Oo's bin chuckin' big dog ends?

MIKE. Where?

BARRY. 'Ardly bin lit.

PETE. 'E's juss waitin' for us t'shift an' 'e'll be on it.

FRED (*holds it out*). On the 'ouse.

MIKE. 'As 'e got a little tin?

COLIN. Like'n ol' tramp?

BARRY. O yeh – 'oo's mindin' the baby?

COLIN (*seeing pram*). Wass that for?

MIKE. Pushin' the spuds in.

FRED (*flicks the dog end to* BARRY). Catch!

COLIN. 'Oo left it 'ere?

BARRY. 'E's takin' it for a walk.

PETE. Nice.

FRED. Piss off.

BARRY. We don't wan' the little nipper t'ear that! Oi, come
  'ere.

COLIN *and* PETE *go to the pram.*

  Oo's 'e look like?

They laugh.

MIKE. Don't stick your ugly mug in its face!

PETE. It'll crap itself t' death.

BARRY. Dad'll change its nappies.

COLIN (*amused*). Bloody nutter!

FRED. You wake it up an' yer can put it t'sleep.

COLIN *and* PETE *laugh.*

BARRY. Put it t'sleep?

COLIN. 'E'll put it t'sleep for good.

PETE. With a brick.

MIKE. 'E don't care if it's awake all night.

BARRY. 'Oo don't? I'm like a bloody uncle t' the kids round
  our way. (*He pushes the pram.*) Doo-dee-doo-dee-doo-dee

MIKE (*to* FRED). Jack it in eh?

FRED. Give 'er another minute.

MIKE. We should a made Len stay with it.

FRED. Slipped up. 'E dodged off bloody sharpish.

MIKE. Sly bleeder.

FRED. I don't know – bloody women!

MIKE. Know a better way?

FRED *and* MIKE *are sitting down left.* PETE *and* COLIN *are right.* BARRY *pushes the pram.*

BARRY.

> Rock a bye baby on a tree top
> When the wind blows the cradle will rock
> When the bough breaks the cradle will fall
> And down will come baby and cradle and tree
>> an' bash its little brains out an' dad'll scoop
>> 'em up and use 'em for bait.

They laugh.

FRED. Save money.

BARRY *takes the balloon. He poses with it.*

COLIN. Thought they was pink now.

BARRY (*pokes at* COLIN'*s head*). Come t' the pictures t'night darlin'? (*He bends it.*) It's got a bend in it.

MIKE. Don't take after its dad.

BARRY (*blows it up*). Ow's that then?

COLIN. Go easy.

BARRY (*blows again*). Thass more like it. (*Blows again.*)

COLIN. Do leave off.

MIKE. That reminds me I said I'd meet the girl t'night.

BARRY *blows. The balloon bursts.*

COLIN. Got me!

He falls dead. BARRY *pushes the pram over him.*

Get off! I'll 'ave a new suit out a you.

BARRY (*pushing the pram round*). Off the same barrer?

PETE. Ain' seen you 'ere before, darlin'.

BARRY. 'Op it!

PETE. 'Ow about poppin' in the bushes?
COLIN. Two's up.
BARRY. What about the nipper?
PETE. Too young for me.

He 'touches' BARRY.

BARRY. 'Ere! Dirty bastard!

He projects the pram viciously after COLIN. *It hits* PETE.

PETE. Bastard!

PETE *and* BARRY *look at each other.* PETE *gets ready to push the pram back – but plays at keeping* BARRY *guessing.* MIKE *and* FRED *are heard talking in their corner.*

MIKE. If there's nothin' in the church, know what?
FRED. No.
MIKE. Do the all-night laundries.
FRED. Yer got a 'and it to yer for tryin'.
MIKE. Yer get all them little 'ousewives there.
FRED. Bit past it though.
MIKE. Yeh, but all right.

PETE *pushes the pram violently at* BARRY. *He catches it straight on the flat of his boot and sends it back with the utmost ferocity.* PETE *sidesteps.* COLIN *stops it.*

PETE. Stupid git!
COLIN. Wass up with 'im?
BARRY. Keep yer dirty 'ands off me!
PETE. 'E'll 'ave the little perisher out!
BARRY. O yeh? An' 'oo reckoned they run a kid down?
PETE. Thass different.
BARRY. Yeh – no one t' see yer.

PETE *pulls the pram from* COLIN, *spins it round and pushes it violently at* BARRY. BARRY *sidesteps and catches it by the handle as it goes past.*

BARRY. Oi – oi!

He looks in the pram.

COLIN. Wass up?

COLIN *and* PETE *come over.*

    It can't open its eyes.

BARRY. Yer woke it.

PETE. Look at its fists.

COLIN. Yeh.

PETE. It's tryin' a clout 'im.

COLIN. Don't blame it.

PETE. Goin' a be a boxer.

BARRY. Is it a girl?

PETE. Yer wouldn't know the difference.

BARRY. 'Ow d'yer get 'em t'sleep?

PETE. Pull their 'air.

COLIN. Eh?

PETE. Like that.

He pulls its hair.

COLIN. That 'urt.

They laugh.

MIKE. Wass 'e doin'?

COLIN. Pullin' its 'air.

FRED. 'E'll 'ave its ol' woman after 'im.

MIKE. Poor sod.

BARRY. 'E's showin' off.

COLIN. 'E wants the coroner's medal.

MIKE (*comes to the pram*). Less see yer do it.

PETE *pulls its hair.*

    O yeh.

BARRY. It don't say nothin'.

COLIN. Little bleeder's 'alf dead a fright.

MIKE. Still awake.
PETE. Ain' co-operatin'.
BARRY. Try a pinch.
MIKE. That ought a work.
BARRY. Like this.

He pinches the baby.

COLIN. Look at that mouth.
BARRY. Flippin' yawn.
PETE. Least it's tryin'.
MIKE. Pull its drawers off.
COLIN. Yeh!
MIKE. Less case its ol' crutch.
PETE. Ha!
BARRY. Yeh!

He throws the nappy in the air.

  Yippee!
COLIN. Look at that!

They laugh.

MIKE. Look at its little legs goin'.
COLIN. Ain' they ugly!
BARRY. Ugh!
MIKE. Can't keep 'em still!
PETE. 'Avin' a fit.
BARRY. It's dirty.

They groan.

COLIN. 'Old its nose.
MIKE. Thass for 'iccups.
BARRY. Gob its crutch.

He spits.

MIKE. Yeh!
COLIN. Ha!

He spits.

MIKE. Got it!

PETE. Give it a punch.

MIKE. Yeh less!

COLIN. There's no one about!

PETE *punches it.*

Ugh! Mind yer don't 'urt it.

MIKE. Yer can't.

BARRY. Not at that age.

MIKE. Course yer can't, no feelin's.

PETE. Like animals.

MIKE. 'It it again.

COLIN. I can't see!

BARRY. 'Arder.

PETE. Yeh.

BARRY. Like that!

He hits it.

COLIN. An' that!

He also hits it.

MIKE. What a giggle!

PETE. Cloutin's good for 'em. I read it.

BARRY (*to* FRED). Why don't you clout it?

FRED. It ain' mine.

PETE. Sherker. Yer got a do yer duty.

FRED. Ain' my worry. Serves 'er right.

BARRY. 'Ere, can I piss on it?

COLIN. Gungy bastard!

MIKE. Got any matches?

They laugh.

PETE. Couldn't yer break them little fingers easy though?

COLIN. Snap!

PETE. Know what they used a do?

MIKE. Yeh.

PETE. Smother 'em.

BARRY. Yeh. That'd be somethin'.

COLIN. Looks like a yeller-nigger.

BARRY. 'Onk like a yid.

FRED. Leave it alone.

PETE. Why?

FRED. Yer don't wan' a row.

PETE. What row?

MIKE. What kid?

COLIN. I ain' seen no kid.

BARRY. Not me!

PETE. Yer wouldn't grass on yer muckers?

FRED. Grow up.

BARRY. D'narf look ill. Stupid bastard.

He jerks the pram violently.

PETE. Thass 'ow they 'ang yer – give yer a jerk.

MIKE. Reckon it'll grow up an idiot.

PETE. Or deformed.

BARRY. Look where it come from.

PETE. Little bleeder.

He jerks the pram violently.

That knocked the grin off its face.

MIKE. Look! Ugh!

BARRY. Look!

COLIN. What?

They all groan.

PETE. Rub the little bastard's face in it!

BARRY. Yeh!

PETE. Less 'ave it!

He rubs the baby. They all groan.

BARRY. Less 'ave a go! I always wan'ed a do that!

PETE. Ain' yer done it before?

BARRY *does it. He laughs.*

COLIN. It's all in its eyes.

Silence.

FRED. There'll be a row.
MIKE. It can't talk.
PETE. 'Oo cares?
FRED. I tol' yer.
COLIN. Shut up.
BARRY. I noticed 'e ain' touched it.
COLIN. Too bloody windy.
FRED. Yeh?
PETE. Less see yer.
BARRY. Yeh.
PETE. 'Fraid she'll ruck yer.
FRED. Ha!

He looks in the pram.

   Chriss.
PETE. Less see yer chuck that.

PETE *throws a stone to* FRED. FRED *doesn't try to catch it. It
falls on the ground.* COLIN *picks it up and gives it to* FRED.

MIKE (*quietly*). Reckon it's all right?
COLIN (*quietly*). No one around.
PETE (*quietly*). They don't know it's us.
MIKE (*quietly*). She left it.
BARRY. It's done now.
PETE (*quietly*). Yer can do what yer like.
BARRY. Might as well enjoy ourselves.
PETE (*quietly*). Yer don't get a chance like this everyday.

FRED *throws the stone.*

COLIN. Missed.
PETE. That ain't'!

He throws a stone.

BARRY. Or that!

He throws a stone.

MIKE. Yeh!
COLIN (*running round*). Where's all the stones?
MIKE (*also running round*). Stick it up the fair!
PETE. Liven 'Ampstead 'eath! Three throws a quid! Make a packet.
MIKE (*throws a stone*). Ouch!
COLIN. 'Ear that?
BARRY. Give us some.

He takes stones from COLIN.

COLIN (*throws a stone*). Right in the lug 'ole.

FRED *looks for a stone.*

PETE. Get its 'ooter.
BARRY. An' its slasher!
FRED (*picks up a stone, spits on it*). For luck, the sod.

He throws.

BARRY. Yyooowwww!
MIKE. 'Ear it plonk!

A bell rings.

MIKE. 'Oo's got the matches?

He finds some in his pocket.

BARRY. What yer doin'?
COLIN. Wan'a buck up!
MIKE. Keep a look out.

He starts to throw burning matches in the pram. BARRY *throws a stone. It just misses* MIKE.

Look out, yer bleedin' git!

COLIN. Guy Fawkes!

PETE. Bloody nutter! Put that out!

MIKE. No! You 'ad what you want!

PETE. Yer'll 'ave the ol' bloody park 'ere!

A bell rings.

BARRY. Piss on it! Piss on it!

COLIN. Gungy slasher.

MIKE. Call the R.S.P.C.A.

A bell rings.

FRED. They'll shut the gates.

PETE (*going*). There's an 'ole in the railin's.

BARRY. 'Old on.

He looks for a stone.

PETE. Leave it!

BARRY. Juss this one!

He throws a stone as PETE *pushes him over. It goes wide.*

Bastard!

To PETE. Yer put me off!

PETE. I'll throttle yer!

BARRY. I got a get it once more!

The others have gone up left. He takes a stone from the pram and throws it at point blank range. Hits.

Yar!

COLIN. Where's this 'ole!

MIKE. Yer bleedin' gear!

FRED. Chriss.

He runs down to the rod and boxes. He picks them up.

BARRY. Bleedin' little sod!

He hacks into the pram. He goes up left.

PETE. Come on!

A bell rings. FRED *has difficulty with the boxes and rod. He throws a box away.*

FRED. 'Ang on!

He goes up left.
They go off up left, making a curious bvzzing. A long pause.
PAM *comes in down left.*

PAM. I might a know'd they'd a left yer. Lucky yer got someone t' look after yer. Muggins 'ere.

She starts to push the pram. She does not look into it. She speaks in a sing-song voice, loudly but to herself.

> 'Oo's 'ad yer balloon. Thass a present from grannie. Goin' a keep me up 'alf the night? Go t' sleepies. Soon be 'ome. Nice an' warm, then. No one else wants yer. Nice an' warm. Soon be 'omies.

SCENE SEVEN

A cell. Left centre a box to sit on. Otherwise, the stage is bare.
A steel door bangs. FRED *comes in from the left. He has a mack over his head. He sits on the case. After a slight pause he takes off the mack.*

Silence. A steel door bangs. PAM *comes in left.*

PAM. What 'appened?
FRED. Didn't yer see 'em?
PAM. I 'eard.

FRED. Bloody 'eathens. Thumpin' and kickin' the van.

PAM. Oo?

FRED. Bloody 'ousewives! 'Oo else? Ought a be stood up an' shot!

PAM. You all right?

FRED. No. I tol' this copper don't open the door. He goes we're 'ere, the thick bastard, an' lets 'em in. Kickin' an' punchin'.

He holds up the mack.

Look at it! Gob all over.

He throws it away from him.

'Course I ain' all right!

Mimicking her. 'Are yer all right?'

PAM. They said I shouldn't be 'ere. But 'e was ever so nice. Said five minutes wouldn't matter.

FRED. Right bloody mess.

PAM. They can't get in 'ere.

FRED. I can't get out there!

PAM. I ain' blamin' yer.

FRED. Blamin' me? Yer got bugger all t'blame me for, mate! Yer ruined my life, thass all!

PAM. I never meant –

FRED. Why the bloody 'ell bring the little perisher out that time a night?

PAM (*fingers at her mouth*). I wanted a –

FRED. Yer got no right chasin' after me with a pram! Drop me right in it!

PAM. I was scared t' stay –

FRED. Never know why yer 'ad the little bleeder in the first place! Yer don't know what yer doin'! Yer're a bloody menace!

PAM. Wass it like?

FRED. They wan' a put you in, then yer'll find out. Bring any burn?

PAM. No.

FRED. Yer don't think a nothin'! Ain' yer got juss one?

PAM. No.

FRED. Yer're bloody useless.

PAM. What'll 'appen!

FRED. 'Ow do I know? I'll be the last one a know. The 'ole thing was an accident. Lot a roughs. Never seen 'em before. Don't arst me. Blokes like that anywhere. I tried to chase 'em off.

PAM. Will they believe that?

FRED. No. If I was ten years older I'd get a medal. With a crowd like our'n they got a knock someone. (*He goes right.*) Right bloody mess.

PAM. Yer never bin in trouble before. Juss one or two woundin's an' that.

FRED. 'Alf murdered with a lot a 'and bags!

PAM. Yer wan' a arst t' see the doctor.

FRED. Doctor! They shouldn't let him touch a sick rat with a barge pole. (*He walks a few steps.*) It's supposed a be grub. A starvin' cat 'ld walk away. (*He walks a few more steps.*) Wass bin 'appening?

PAM. Don't know.

FRED. On yer own?

PAM. What about them others?

FRED. What about 'em?

PAM. I could say I saw 'em.

FRED. That'd make it worse. Don't worry. I'm thinkin' it all out. This way they don't know what 'appened. Not definite. Why couldn't I bin tryin' a 'elp the kid? I got no cause t' 'arm it.

He sits on the box.

PAM. I tol' 'em.

FRED (*he puts his arms round her waist and leans his head against her*). Yer'll 'ave t' send us letters.

PAM. I'm buyin' a pad on me way 'ome.

FRED. Pam. I don't know what'll 'appen. There's bloody gangs like that roamin' everywhere. The bloody police don't do their job.

PAM. I'll kill meself if they touch yer.

A steel door bangs. LEN *comes in left.*

I tol' yer t' wait outside.

LEN. I got 'im some fags. (*To* FRED.) I 'ad a drop 'em 'alf.

PAM. 'E still won't leave me alone, Fred.

LEN. I only got a minute. They're arstin' for a remand.

FRED. Chriss. That bloody mob still outside?

LEN. They've 'emmed 'em off over the road.

FRED. Bit bloody late.

PAM. Tell 'im t' go.

LEN. We both got a go. That inspector wants you.

FRED. Where's the snout?

LEN. Put it in yer pocket.

FRED (*to* PAM). See yer after.

She puts her arms round him before he can take the cigarettes.

PAM. I'll wait for yer.

FRED (*pats her back*). Yeh, yeh. God 'elp us.

LEN (*to* PAM). Yer'll get 'im into trouble if yer don't go.

FRED *nods at* PAM. *She goes out crying.*

FRED. 'Ow many yer got?

LEN. Sixty. I 'ad a drop 'em 'alf.

FRED. Will it be all right?

LEN. Give 'em a few like, an' don't flash 'em around.

FRED. She never 'ad none. I'll do the same for you sometime.

LEN. Put 'em in yer pocket.

FRED. I don't know what I'll get.

LEN. Manslaughter. (*Shrugs.*) Anythin'.

FRED. It was only a kid.

LEN. I saw.

FRED. What?

LEN. I come back when I couldn't find 'er.

FRED. Yer ain't grassed?

LEN. No.

FRED. O.

LEN. I was in the trees. I saw the pram.

FRED. Yeh.

LEN. I saw the lot.

FRED. Yeh.

LEN. I didn't know what t'do. Well, I should a stopped yer.

FRED. Too late now.

LEN. I juss saw.

FRED. Yer saw! Yer saw! Wass the good a that? That don't
'elp me. I'll be out in that bloody dock in a minute!

LEN. Nothin'. They got the pram in court.

FRED. Okay, okay. Reckon there's time for a quick burn?

LEN. About.

He gives FRED *a light.*

INTERVAL

SCENE EIGHT

The living-room.

HARRY *irons,* LEN *sits.*

LEN. Yer make a fair ol' job a that.

Pause.

  Don't yer get choked off?

HARRY. What?

LEN. That every Friday night.
HARRY. Got a keep clean.
LEN. Suppose so.

Pause.

Yer get used t' it.
HARRY. Trained to it in the army.
LEN. O.
HARRY. Makes a man a yer.

MARY *comes in. She looks around.*

MARY *to* LEN. I wish yer wouldn't sit around in yer ol' work-clothes an' shoes. Yer got some nice slippers.

MARY *goes out.*

LEN. She won't let Pam.
HARRY. Eh?
LEN. She won't let Pam do that for yer.
HARRY. Don't take me long.

Long pause.

LEN. Yer could stop 'er money.

Slight pause.

Then she couldn't interfere.
HARRY. Don't take long. Once yer get started.
LEN. Why don't yer try that?
HARRY. That Pam can't iron. She'd ruin 'em.
LEN. Ever thought a movin' on?
HARRY. This stuff gets dry easy.
LEN. Yer ought a think about it.
HARRY. Yer don't know what yer talking about, lad.
LEN. No. I don't.
HARRY. It's like everthin' else.
LEN. 'Ow long yer bin 'ere?

HARRY. Don't know. (*He stretches his back. He irons again.*) Yer mate's comin' out.

LEN. Yeh. Why?

HARRY. Pam's mate. (*He spits on the iron.*) None a it ain' simple.

LEN. Yer lost a little boy eh?

HARRY. Next week, ain't it?

LEN. I got a shirt yer can do. (*Laughs.*) Any offers?

HARRY. She meet 'im?

LEN. Ain' arst.

HARRY. You?

LEN (*shrugs*). I'd 'ave t' get time off.

HARRY. O.

LEN. 'Ow d'yer get on at work?

HARRY (*looks up*). It's a job.

LEN. I meant with the blokes?

HARRY (*irons*). They're all right.

LEN. Funny, nightwork.

PAM *comes in. She has her hair in a towel. She carries a portable radio. Someone is talking. She sits on the couch and finds a pop programme. She tunes in badly. She interrupts this from time to time to rub her hair.*

LEN (*to* HARRY). 'Ow about doin' my shirt?

He laughs. PAM *finishes tuning. She looks round.*

PAM. 'Oo's got my *Radio Times*? You 'ad it?

HARRY *doesn't answer. She turns to* LEN.

You?

LEN (*mumbles*). Not again.

PAM. You speakin' t' me?

LEN. I'm sick t' death a yer bloody *Radio Times*.

PAM. Someone's 'ad it. (*She rubs her hair vigorously.*) I ain' goin' a get it no more. Not after last week. I'll cancel it. It's the last time I bring it in this 'ouse. I don't see why I

'ave t' go on paying for it. Yer must think I'm made a
money. It's never 'ere when I wan'a see it. Not once. It's
always the same. (*She rubs her hair.*) I notice no one else
offers t' pay for it. Always Charlie. It's 'appened once too
often this time.

LEN. Every bloody week the same!

PAM (*to* HARRY). Sure yer ain' got it?

HARRY. I bought this shirt over eight years ago.

PAM. That cost me sixpence a week. You reckon that up over
a year. Yer must think I was born yesterday.

Pause. She rubs her hair.

Wasn't 'ere last week. Never 'ere. Got legs.

She goes to the door and shouts.

Mum! She 'eard all right.

She goes back to the couch and sits. She rubs her hair.

Someone's got it. I shouldn't think the people next door
come in an' took it. Everyone 'as the benefit a it 'cept me.
It's always the same. I'll know what t' do in future. Two
can play at that game. I ain' blinkin' daft. (*She rubs her hair.*)
I never begrudge no one borrowin' it, but yer'd think they'd
have enough manners t' put it back.

Pause.

She rubs her hair.

Juss walk all over yer. Well it ain' goin' a 'appen again.
They treat you like a door mat. All take and no give. Touch
somethin' a their'n an' they go through the bloody ceilin'.
It's bin the same ever since –

LEN. I tol' yer t' keep it in yer room!

PAM. Now yer got a lock things up in yer own 'ouse.

LEN. Why should we put up with this week after week juss
    because yer too –

PAM. Yer know what yer can do.

LEN. Thass yer answer t' everythin'.

PAM. Got a better one?

HARRY. They was a pair first off. Set me back a quid each. Up the market. One's gone 'ome, went at the cuffs. Worth a quid.

LEN. Chriss.

Pause.

PAM. I mean it this time. I'm goin' in that shop first thing Saturday mornin' an' tell 'im t' cancel it. I ain' throwin' my money down the drain juss to –

LEN. Wrap up!

PAM. Don't tell me what t' do!

LEN. Wrap up!

PAM. Thass typical a you.

She goes to the door and calls. Mum!

To LEN. I ain' stupid. I know 'oo's got it.

Calls. Mum! – She can 'ear.

HARRY. Ain' worth readin' any'ow.

LEN. Don't start 'er off again.

PAM (*to* LEN). You ain' sittin' on it, a course!

LEN. No.

PAM. Yer ain' looked.

LEN. Ain' goin' to.

PAM. 'Ow d'yer know yer ain' sittin' on it?

LEN. I ain' sittin' on it.

PAM (*to* HARRY). Tell 'im t' get up!

HARRY. Waste a good money.

PAM (*to* LEN). Yer'll be sorry for this.

LEN. I'll be sorry for a lot a things.

HARRY. Cuffs goin' on this one.

PAM (*by* LEN's *chair*). I ain' goin' till yer move.

HARRY. Lot a lies an' pictures a nancies.

PAM. Yer dead spiteful when yer wan'a be.

LEN. Thass right.

PAM (*goes to the couch, rubbing her hair*). 'E'oo laughs last. Fred's coming 'ome next week.

LEN. 'Ome?

PAM. 'Is ol' lady won't 'ave 'im in the 'ouse.

LEN. Where's 'e goin'?

PAM. Yer'll see.

LEN. 'E ain' 'avin' my room.

PAM. 'Oo said?

LEN. She won't let yer.

PAM. We'll see.

LEN. Yer ain' even arst 'er.

PAM. O no?

LEN. No.

PAM (*rubs her hair*). We'll see.

LEN. I'll 'ave one or two things t' say. Yer too fond a pushin' people about.

PAM. Must take after you.

LEN. I thought 'e'd be sharin' your room.

PAM. I ain' rowin' about it. 'E'll 'ave t' 'ave somewhere t' come out to. Chriss knows what it's like shut up in them places. It'll be nice an' clean 'ere for 'im when yer're gone.

LEN. 'Ave yer arst 'im yet?

PAM. I ain' rowin' about it. If 'e goes wanderin' off 'e'll only end up in trouble again. I ain' goin' a be messed around over this! We ain' gettin' any younger. 'E's bound a be different. (*She rubs her hair.*) Yer can't say anythin' in letters. Yer can't expect 'im to.

LEN. 'Ave yer arst 'im.

PAM. I don' wan' a talk about it.

LEN. You meetin' 'im?

PAM. Why? – You ain' comin'!

LEN. 'Oo said?

PAM. 'E don't want you there!

LEN. 'Ow d'yer know?

PAM. O let me alone!

LEN. 'E's my mate, ain' 'e?

PAM. I'm sick t' death a you under me feet all the time! Ain'
yer got no friends t' go to! What about yer people? Won't
they take yer in either?

LEN. Yer arst some stupid questions at times.

PAM. Yer can't 'ave no pride. Yer wouldn't catch me 'angin'
round where I ain' wanted.

LEN. 'Oo ain' wanted?

PAM. I don't want yer! They don't want yer! It's only common
sense! I don't know why yer can't see it. It's nothin' but rows
an' arguments.

LEN. 'Oo's fault's that?

PAM. Anybody else wouldn't stay if yer paid 'em! Yer caused
all the trouble last time.

LEN. I knew that was comin'.

PAM. None a that 'ld a 'appened if yer ain' bin 'ere. Yer never
give 'im a chance.

LEN. Yeh, yeh.

PAM. Yer live on trouble!

LEN. That ain' what 'e told everyone.

PAM. Same ol' lies.

LEN. Listen 'oo's talkin'!

PAM. Yer start off gettin' 'im put away –

LEN. Don't be bloody stupid!

PAM. Jealous! An' now 'e's comin' out yer still can't let 'im
alone!

LEN. *You* can't leave 'im alone yer mean!

PAM. Yer laughed yer 'ead off when they took 'im away.

LEN. Bloody stupid! You arst 'im!

PAM. Comin' 'ere an' workin' me up!

LEN. Yer wan'a listen t' yerself!

PAM. So do you.

LEN. Shoutin'.

PAM. 'Oo's shoutin'?

LEN. You are!

PAM. Yer 'ave t' shout with you!

LEN. Thass right!

PAM. Yer so bloody dense!

LEN. Go on!

PAM. Yer 'ave t' shout!

LEN. Yer silly bloody cow!

PAM. Shoutin' 'e says! 'Ark at 'im! 'Ark at 'im!

LEN. Shut up!

PAM. We ain' carryin' on like this! Yer got a stop upsettin' me night after night!

LEN. You start it!

PAM. It's got a stop! It ain' worth it! Juss round an' round.

A very long silence.

Yer can't say it's the kid keepin' yer.

A long silence.

It certainly ain' me. Thass well past.

Silence.

Yer sit there in yer dirty ol' work clothes. (*To* HARRY.) Why don't yer turn 'im out? Dad.

HARRY. 'E pays 'is rent.

PAM. Fred'll pay.

HARRY. 'As 'e got a job?

PAM. 'E'll get one.

HARRY. Will 'e keep it?

PAM. Thass right!

LEN. Now 'oo's startin' it?

PAM. You are.

LEN. I ain' said a word.

PAM. No – but yer sat there!

LEN. I got some rights yer know!

PAM. Yer're juss like a kid.

LEN. I'm glad I ain' yourn.

PAM. I wouldn't like t' 'ave your spiteful nature.

LEN. I certainly wouldn't like yourn!

PAM. Thass right! I know why yer sittin' there!

LEN. Yer know a sight bloody too much!

PAM. I know where my *Radio Times* is!

LEN. Stick yer bloody *Radio Times*!

PAM. I know why yer sittin' there!

LEN. That bloody paper!

PAM. Why don't yer stand up?

LEN. Yer don't even want the bloody paper!

PAM. As long as yer causin' trouble –

LEN. Yer juss wan' a row!

PAM. – then yer're 'appy!

LEN. If yer found it yer'd lose somethin' else!

PAM (*goes to* LEN's *chair*). Stand up then!

LEN. No!

PAM. Can't it a got there accidentally?

LEN. No!

PAM. Yer see!

LEN. I ain' bein' pushed around.

PAM. Yer see!

LEN. Yer come too much a it!

PAM. No yer'd rather stay stuck!

LEN. A sight bloody too much!

PAM. An' row!

LEN. Shut up!

PAM. Thass right!

LEN. I tol' yer t' shut up!

PAM. Go on!

LEN. Or I'll bloody well shut yer up!

PAM. O yeh!

LEN. Yer need a bloody good beltin'.

PAM. Touch me!

LEN. You started this!

PAM. Go on!

LEN (*he turns away*). Yer make me sick!

PAM. Yeh – yer see. Yer make me sick!

She goes to the door.

I ain' lettin' a bloody little weed like you push me around!
Calls. Mum.

She comes back.

I wish I 'ad a record a when yer first come 'ere. Butter
wouldn't melt in yer mouth.

Calls. Mum!

HARRY (*finishing ironing*). Thass that, thank Chriss.

PAM (*calls*). Mum! – She can' 'ear.

Calls. You 'eard?

HARRY. Put the wood in the 'ole.

LEN. I'd like t' 'ear what they're sayin' next door.

PAM. Let 'em say!

LEN. 'Ole bloody neighbour'ood must know!

PAM. Good – let 'em know what yer're like!

LEN. 'Oo wen' on about pride?

PAM (*calls through door*). I know yer can' 'ear.

MARY (*off*). You callin' Pam?

PAM (*to* LEN). One thing, anythin' else goes wrong I'll know
'oo t' blame.

MARY (*off*). Pam!

PAM. Let 'er wait.

MARY (*off.*) Pam!

LEN (*calls*). It's all right! One a 'er fits!

PAM (*calls*). 'E's sittin' on the chair.

MARY (*off*). What?

PAM (*calls*). 'E's got my paper!

MARY (*off*). What chair?

PAM (*calls*). 'E 'as!

MARY (*off*). I ain' got yer paper!

PAM (*calls*). It don't matter!

MARY (*off*). What paper's that?

PAM (*calls*). It don't matter! You bloody deaf?

LEN. Now start on 'er!

HARRY (*piling his clothes neatly*). Didn't take long.

PAM (*to* LEN). Yer're so bloody clever!

LEN. If I upset yer like this why don't *you* go?

PAM. Thass what you want!

LEN (*shrugs*). You want *me* t' go!

PAM. I ain' bein' pushed out on no streets.

LEN. I'm tryin' t' 'elp.

PAM. Yer wouldn't 'elp a cryin' baby.

LEN. Yer're the last one a bring that up!

PAM. 'Elp? – after the way yer carried on t'night.

LEN. I lost me job stayin' out a 'elp you when yer was sick!

PAM. Sacked for bein' bloody lazy!

LEN (*stands*). Satisfied?

PAM (*without looking at the chair*). Yer torn it up or burnt it!
    Wouldn't put that pass yer!

PAM *goes out. Silence.* HARRY *finishes folding his clothes.*

MARY (*off*). Found it yet?

Pause.

HARRY. Wan'a use it?

LEN. No.

HARRY *folds the board.*

SCENE NINE

The living-room.
LEN *has spread a paper on the floor. He cleans his shoes on it.*
MARY *comes in. She is in her slip. She walks about getting ready.*

MARY. 'Ope yer don't mind me like this.

LEN. You kiddin'?

MARY. It's such a rush. I don't really wan'a go.

LEN. Don't then.

MARY. I said I would now.

LEN. Say yer don't feel up to it.

MARY. Yes. (*She goes on getting ready.*) Makes a change I suppose.

LEN. Never know, it might be a laugh.

MARY. Yer got a do somethin' t' entertain yerself.

Pause.

I 'ope yer ain' usin' 'er *Radio Times*.

LEN. Ha!

MARY. She's got no patience. It'll land 'er in trouble one a these days. Look at that pram. I told 'er t'wait. She should a got two 'undred for that.

LEN. Easy.

MARY (*looks at her shoes*). This ain' nice. No, she 'as t' let it go for fifty quid, the first time she's arst. Can't be told. Yer couldn't give these a little touch up for me?

LEN. Sling 'em over.

MARY. Ta, dear.

LEN. What yer put on these?

MARY. That white stuff.

LEN *polishes her shoes in silence.*

Thinkin'?

LEN. No.

MARY. Whass worryin' yer?

LEN. Nothin'.

MARY. I expect yer're like me. Yer enjoy the quiet. I don't enjoy all this noise yer get.

LEN. She said somethin' about my room?

MARY (*amused*). Why?

LEN. What she say?

MARY. That worried yer?

LEN. I ain' worried.

MARY. She's not tellin' me 'ow t' run my 'ouse.

She pulls on her stockings.

LEN. O. (*Holds up her shoes.*) Do yer?

MARY. Very nice. Juss go over the backs dear. I like t' feel nice be'ind. I tol' 'er there's enough t' put up with without lookin' for trouble.

LEN. Better?

MARY. Yes. I 'ad enough a that pair last time.

She steps into one shoe.

We're only goin' for the big film. She can do what she likes outside.

LEN (*gives her the other shoe*). Thass yer lot.

MARY. 'E wants lockin' up for life. Ta, dear. I don't expect yer t' understand at your age, but things don't turn out too bad. There's always someone worse off in the world.

LEN (*clearing up the polishing things*). Yer can always be that one.

MARY. She's my own flesh an' blood, but she don't take after me. Not a thought in 'er 'ead. She's 'ad a rough time a it. I feel sorry for 'er about the kid –

LEN. One a them things. Yer can't make too much a it.

MARY. Never 'ave 'appened if she'd a look after it right. Yer done a lovely job on these. What yer doin' t'night?

LEN (*sews a button on his shirt*). Gettin' ready for work.

MARY. Yer don't go out so much.

LEN. I was out Tuesday.

MARY. Yer ought a be out every night.

LEN. Can't afford it.

MARY. There's plenty a nice girls round 'ere.

LEN. I ain' got the energy these days. They want – somethin' flash.

MARY. Yer can't tell me what they want. I was the same that age.

LEN. I ain' got time for 'alf a 'em. They don't know what they got it for.

MARY. I thought that's what you men were after.

LEN. 'Alf a 'em, it ain' worth the bother a gettin' there. Thass a fact.

MARY. What about the other 'alf?

LEN. Hm!

MARY (*having trouble with her suspender*). Yer 'ave t' go about it the right way. Yer can't stand a girl in a puddle down the back a some ol' alley an' think yer doin' 'er a favour. Yer got yer own room upstairs. That's a nice room. Surprised yer don't use that. I don't mind what goes on, yer know that. As long as yer keep the noise down.

LEN. Ta.

MARY. It's in every man. It 'as t' come out.

Pause.

We didn't carry on like that when I was your age.

LEN. Pull the other one.

MARY. Not till yer was in church. Anyway, yer 'ad t' be engaged. I think it's nicer in the open. I do.

LEN. I bet yer bin up a few alleys.

MARY. You enjoy yerself. I know what I'd be doin' if I was you.

LEN. You meetin' a fella?

MARY. No! I'm goin' out with Mrs Lee.

LEN. Waste.

MARY. Don't be cheeky.

LEN. Yer look fair when yer all done up.

MARY. What you after? Bin spendin' me rent money?

LEN. Wass on?

MARY. Don't know. Somethin' daft.

LEN. Shall I look it up?

MARY. They're all the same. Sex. Girls 'angin' out a their dresses an' men bendin' over 'em.

LEN. It's one of them nudes. 'Eard the fellas talkin'.

MARY. Shan't go in.

LEN. Don't know what yer missin'.

MARY. Different for men.

LEN. Always full a tarts when I bin.

MARY. Thass where yer spend yer money.

LEN. Very nice. Big ol' tits bouncin' about in sinner-scope.

MARY. Don't think Mrs Lee'd fancy that.

LEN. I'll 'ave t' take yer one a these nights.

MARY. I'd rather see Tarzan.

LEN. Thass easy, come up next time I 'ave a bath.

MARY. Count the 'airs on yer chest?

LEN. For a start.

MARY. Sounds like a 'orror film.

LEN. I enjoy a good scrub. On me back.

MARY. Thass the regular carry-on in China.

LEN. No 'arm in it.

MARY. No.

Slight pause.

Pam's very easy goin' for a nice girl. I suppose yer miss that.

LEN. Takes a bit a gettin' used to.

MARY. 'Ow'd yer manage?

LEN. Any suggestions?

Slight pause.

MARY. Bugger!

LEN. Eh?

MARY. Thass tore it!

LEN. Wass up?

MARY. O blast! I caught me stockin'.

LEN. O.

MARY. That would 'ave to 'appen.

LEN. 'Ow'd yer do it?

MARY. Juss when I'm late. Bugger it.

She looks in the table drawer.

'Ardly worth goin' in a minute. Excuse my language. Never find anythin' when yer want it in this place.

LEN. What yer lost?

MARY. It's the only decent pair I got.

LEN. Thass a shame.

MARY. It'll run.

LEN. Less 'ave a shufties.

MARY. Caught on that blasted chair. It's bin like that for ages.

LEN. Yeh. Thass a big one.

MARY. Pam's got 'er nail-varnish all over the place except when yer wan'a find it.

LEN (*offers her the needle*). 'Ave a loan of this.

MARY. It'll run, y'see.

LEN. Less do the cotton.

MARY. I certainly can't afford new ones this week.

LEN (*threading the needle*). Not t' worry.

MARY. I'm no good at that.

LEN. Well, 'ave a bash.

MARY. It'll make it worse.

LEN. No it won't.

MARY (*puts her foot on the chair seat*). You do it.

LEN. Me?

MARY. I never could use a needle. I should a bin there by now.

LEN. I don't know if I –

MARY. Get on. It's only doin' me a good turn.

LEN. It ain' that. I –

MARY. Mrs Lee's waitin'. I can't take 'em off. I'm in ever such a 'urry. They'll run.

LEN. Yeh. It's dodgy. I don't wan'a prick –

MARY. Yer got steady 'ands your age.

LEN (*kneels in front of her and starts darning*). Yeh. (*He drops the needle*). O.

MARY. All right?

LEN. It's dropped.

MARY. What?

LEN. Me needle.

MARY. Yer're 'oldin' me up.

LEN (*on his hands and knees*). 'Ang on.

MARY. That it?

LEN. No.

MARY (*she helps him to look*). Can't a got far.

LEN. It's gone.

MARY. What's that?

LEN. Where?

MARY. That's it. There.

LEN. O. Ta.

MARY (*puts her foot back on the chair*). I ain' got all night.

LEN. I'll 'ave t' get me 'and inside.

MARY. You watch where yer go. Yer ain' on yer 'oneymoon
yet. Yer 'and's cold!

LEN. Keep still, or it'll jab yer.

MARY. You watch yerself.

LEN. I'll juss give it a little stretch.

MARY. All right?

LEN. Yer got lovely legs.

MARY. You get on with it.

LEN. Lovely an' smooth.

MARY. Never mind my legs.

LEN. It's a fact.

MARY. Some people'd 'ave a fit if they 'eard that. Yer know
what they're like.

LEN. Frustrated.

MARY. I'm old enough t' be yer mother.

HARRY *comes in. He goes straight to the table.*

To LEN. Go steady!

LEN. Sorry.

MARY. You watch where yer pokin'. That 'urt.

LEN. I tol' yer t' keep still.

MARY. Yer'll make it bigger, not smaller.

HARRY *takes ink and a Pools coupon from the table drawer. He puts them on the table.*

LEN. That'll see yer through t'night.

He ties a knot in the thread.

MARY. Wass up now?

LEN. Scissors.

MARY. Eh?

LEN. I 'ad 'em juss now.

MARY. Bite it.

LEN. Eh?

MARY. Go on.

LEN (*leans forward*). Keep still.

MARY. I can't wait all night.

LEN *bites the thread off.* HARRY *goes out.*

Took yer time.

LEN (*stands*). Ow! I'm stiff.

MARY (*looks*). Ta, very nice.

LEN. Ain' worth goin' now.

MARY. 'Ave I got me cigarettes?

LEN. Might be somethin' on telly.

MARY. I can't disappoint Mrs Lee.

LEN. I 'ad a feelin' 'e'd come in.

MARY. Yer'll be in bed time I get back.

LEN. She won't wait this long.

MARY. I'll say good night. Thanks for 'elpin'.

LEN. Stay in an' put yer feet up. I'll make us a cup of tea.

MARY. Can't let yer friends down. Cheerio.

LEN. Okay.

MARY *goes.* LEN *takes a handkerchief from his pocket. He switches the light off and goes to the couch.*

SCENE TEN

A café.
Furniture: chairs and three tables, one up right, one right and one down left. Apart from this the stage is bare.

LEN *and* PAM *sit at the table up right.*

LEN (*drinks tea*). Warms yer up.

Pause.

These early mornin's knock me out. 'Nother cup?

Pause.

PAM. Wass the time?
LEN. Quarter past.
PAM. Why ain't they got a clock?

Pause.

LEN. 'Ave another one.
PAM. Thass the fourth time yer keep arstin.
LEN. Warm yer up.
PAM. Go an' sit on yer own table.

Pause.

LEN. Sure yer wrote the name right?
PAM. We'll look bloody daft when 'e finds you 'ere. Wass 'e goin' to say?
LEN. 'Ello.

Pause.

Let me go an' find 'im.
PAM. No.
LEN. There's no use –

PAM. No!

LEN. Suit yerself.

PAM. Do I 'ave t' say everythin' twice?

LEN. There's no need t' shout.

PAM. I ain' shoutin'.

LEN. They can 'ear yer 'alf way t' –

PAM. I don't wan'a know.

LEN. Yer never do.

Silence.

PAM. Len. I don't want a keep on at yer. I don't know what's the matter with me. They wan'a put the 'eat on. It's like death. Yer'd get on a lot better with someone else.

LEN. Per'aps 'e ain' comin'.

PAM. They must 'ave all the winders open. It's no life for a fella. Yer ain' a bad sort.

LEN. Yeh. I'm goin' a be late in.

PAM. Don't go.

LEN. You make me money up?

PAM *(after a slight pause).* Why can't yer go somewhere?

LEN. Where?

PAM. There's lots a places.

LEN. 'Easy t' say.

PAM. I'll find yer somewhere.

LEN. I ain' scuttlin' off juss t' make room for you t' shag in.

PAM. Yer're a stubborn sod! Don't blame me what 'appens t' yer! Yer ain' messin' me about again.

LEN. I knew that wouldn't last long!

PAM. I'm sick t' death a yer. Clear off!

She goes to the table down left and sits. LEN *goes out left. Pause. He comes back with a cup of tea. He puts it on the table in front of* PAM. *He stands near the table.*

LEN. It'll get cold.

Pause.

Did 'e say 'e'd come?

Pause.

Did 'e answer any a your letters?

She re-acts.

I juss wondered!
PAM. I tol' yer before!
LEN. Thass all right then.

Pause.

PAM. It's like winter in 'ere.

There are voices off right. Someone shouts. A door bangs open.
MIKE, COLIN, PETE, BARRY, FRED *and* LIZ *come in.*

COLIN. 'Ere we are again.
BARRY. Wipe yer boots.
MIKE. On you!
BARRY. Where we sittin'?
MIKE. On yer 'ead.
BARRY. On me arse!
LIZ. Don't know 'ow 'e tells the difference.

She laughs.

FRED. This'll do.
PETE. All right?
LIZ. Can I sit 'ere?
MIKE. Sit where yer like, dear.
BARRY. What we 'avin'?
PETE (*to* FRED). What yer fancy?
FRED. What they got?
PETE (*looks left*). Double egg, bacon, 'am, bangers, double
    bangers, sper-gety –
BARRY. Chips.
FRED. Juss bring the lot.

PETE. Oi, ease off.

FRED. An' four cups a tea.

PETE. I'm standin' yer for this!

FRED. Make that twice.

BARRY. An' me!

PETE (*to* LIZ). Wass yourn, darlin'?

FRED. Now or later?

PETE. Now, t' start with.

BARRY. Tea and crumpet.

LIZ. Could I 'ave a coffee?

FRED. 'Ave what yer like, darlin'.

BARRY. Cup a tea do me!

COLIN. Wass she 'avin' later!

LIZ. Dinner.

MIKE. Teas all round then.

BARRY. Right.

MIKE (*to* FRED). Sit down, we'll fix it.

PETE, MIKE *and* COLIN *go off left.*

FRED. Where's all the burn?

LIZ. I only got one left.

FRED (*calls*). Get us some snout.

MIKE. Five or ten?

FRED *makes a rude gesture.* LIZ *offers him her cigarette.*

FRED. Keep it, darlin'. I'm okay.

He turns to LEN *and* PAM. Oi, 'ello then. 'Ow's it goin'?

He stands and goes down to their table. LEN *has already sat.*

PAM. 'Ello.

FRED. Thass right, yer said yer'd be 'ere. (*Calls.*) That grub
ready? (*To* PAM.) Yeh.

BARRY (*to* FRED). Big gut!

COLIN (*off*). Give us a chance!

PETE (*off*). They didn't teach yer no manners inside.

FRED. Yer're arstin' for trouble. I don't wan'a go back juss yet.

PAM. You all right?

FRED. Yeh. You look all right.

LIZ. Don't yer reckon 'e looks thin?

PAM. I can't –

LIZ. Like a rake. I tol' yer, didn't I? Yer wan'a get some meat on yer.

FRED. I will when that grub turns up.

BARRY *and* LIZ *are sitting at the table up right.* BARRY *bangs the table.*

BARRY. Grub!

COLIN (*off*). Ease up, louse!

BARRY (*calls*). Make that two coffees. (*He puts on an accent.*) I feel like a cup.

LIZ. Ain' what yer sound like.

PETE (*off*). Shut 'im up!

BARRY *makes a gesture.*

FRED. Why did the policewoman marry the 'angman?

LIZ. Eh?

FRED. They both liked necking.

They laugh.

PETE (*off*). Why was the undertaker buried alive?

LIZ. 'Is job got on top a 'im.

They laugh.

BARRY. Why did the woman with three tits 'ave quads?

MIKE. We 'eard it!

The rest groan.

COLIN (*off*). What about the sailor 'oo drowned in 'is bath?

FRED. 'Is brother was the fireman 'oo went up in smoke.

They laugh.

PETE (*off*). Didn't know they let yer 'ave jokes inside.

LIZ. Wass it like?

FRED. In there?

LIZ. Yeh.

FRED (*shrugs. To* LEN). 'Ow's the job?

LEN. Stinks.

FRED. It don't change. (*He sits at their table.*) Long time.

LIZ. Got a light?

FRED (*to* PAM). I got yer letters didn't I.

PAM. Yeh.

FRED. I ain' good at writin'.

PETE, COLIN *and* MIKE *shout and laugh, off.*

PAM. Where yer goin'?

FRED. I'm goin' to 'ave the biggest nosh-up a me life.

BARRY (*to* FRED). Did yer be'ave yerself inside?

PAM (*to* FRED). No, after that.

FRED. O yer know.

PAM. Yer fixed up?

FRED. 'Ow?

PAM. I'll take yer roun' our place.

FRED. O –

LEN. Yer can muck in with me a couple a nights. Give yerself
time t' get straight.

FRED. Ta, I don't wan' a put –

LEN. Yer won't be in the way for a couple of days.

PAM. Mum'll shut up. It'll be nice and quiet. Thass what
yer need.

FRED. Yer must be kidding!

BARRY (*to* LIZ). Arst 'im if 'e be'aved isself.

LIZ (*to* FRED). 'Ear that?

FRED. Yer know me.

BARRY. Not 'arf.

FRED. One day.

LIZ. Yeh.

FRED. This padre 'as me in.

BARRY. O yeh.

FRED. Wants t' chat me up. 'E says nothin that comes out a
a man can be all bad.

BARRY. Whass that?

FRED. Then 'e 'ops out an' I 'as a little slash in 'is tea.

LIZ *and* BARRY *laugh –* LIZ *very loudly.*

LIZ. What 'appened?

FRED. 'E reckoned they ain' put the sugar in.

They laugh.

Another bloke –

LIZ. Yeh.

FRED. Stares at me. Keeps starin' at me. All day. It's 'is first
day, see.

BARRY. Go on.

FRED. So I gets 'im on the landin' an' clobbers 'im.

BARRY. Bang!

FRED. An' it only turns out 'e'd got a squint!

They laugh.

LIZ. Wass it like inside?

FRED. I got chokey for the clobberin'. Bread and water!

BARRY. On yer jack.

FRED. Only good thing there's no one t' scrounge yer grub.

BARRY. Yer d'narf tell 'em.

FRED. Ain' my sort a life. Glad I done it once, but thass their
lot. Ain' pinnin' nothin' on me next time.

LIZ. Wass it like?

FRED. In there?

LIZ. Yeh.

FRED. Cold.

LIZ. Eh?

FRED. Cold.

Silence. MIKE *comes in a few paces from the left.*

MIKE. Won't be 'alf a jik.

FRED. 'Bout time.

COLIN (*off*). 'E still moanin'?

COLIN *comes on and stands with* MIKE.

FRED. Eh?

COLIN. Bet yer couldn't carry-on in there.

FRED. Lot I couldn't do in there, if yer like t' look at it.

MIKE. We ain' got a treat yer everyday.

FRED. I'll pay for this if you like. (*To* LIZ.) Lend us ten bob.

PETE *comes in.*

PETE. 'Oo arst yer t' pay?

FRED. I reckon it's worth one lousy meal.

PETE. Yer made yer own decisions, didn't yer?

BARRY (*comes down*). Wass up?

PETE. We ain' got a crawl up yer arse.

COLIN. Grub smell all right, don't –

PETE. 'Ang on a minute, Col.

MIKE (*to* PETE). Nah, it's 'is first day out, Pete. Let 'im settle down.

COLIN. Come on.

He starts to go left.

PETE. 'E ain' swingin' that one on me.

PETE *and* COLIN *go out left.*

MIKE (*to* FRED). 'E got out the wrong bed this mornin'.

MIKE *follows them off. Slight pause.*

FRED (*laughs*). It's the ol' lag comin' out a me! (*Shouts.*) Whoopee!

BARRY. Ha-ha! Whoopee!

FRED.

> She was only a goalkeeper's daughter
> She married a player called Jack

It was great when 'e played centre forward
But 'e liked to slip round to the back.
(*He laughs.*) I used a lie in me pit thinkin' a that.

COLIN (*off*): What?

FRED: Nosh.

LIZ. That all?

FRED. An' tryin' a remember whass up your legs.

LIZ. I'll draw yer a picture. Give us a light.

FRED (*to* PAM). Give 'er a light.

He gives her a box of matches. She takes them to LIZ. *To*
LEN. Wass 'er game?

LEN. I don't wan'a get involved, mate.

FRED. Yeh? Yer should a read them crummy letters she
keeps sendin'. She ain' goin' a catch me round 'er place.

LEN. No. What was it like?

FRED. No, talk about somethin' else.

LEN. No, *before*.

FRED. Yer 'eard the trial.

PAM *comes back to the table.*

Go away, Pam.

PAM. I wan' a finish me tea.

LEN. Thass cold.

FRED. Can't yer take a 'int? Take yer tea over there.

PAM. Wass goin' on?

LEN. Nothin'!

FRED. No one's talkin' about you.

PAM (*going to sit down at the table*). I'd rather –

FRED. O Pam!

She goes to the unoccupied table and watches them.

'Er ol' people still alive? If yer can call it that.

LEN. Yeh.

FRED. Yer ain' still livin' there?

LEN. I'm goin' soon.

FRED. Yer're as bad as them. She won't get me there in a
  month a Sundays.

LEN. What was it like?

FRED. I tol' yer.

LEN. No, before.

FRED. Before what?

LEN. In the park.

FRED. Yer saw.

LEN. Wass it feel like?

FRED. Don't know.

LEN. When yer was killin' it.

FRED. Do what?

LEN. Wass it feel like when yer killed it?

BARRY (*to* LIZ). Fancy a record?

LIZ. Wouldn't mind.

BARRY. Give us a tanner then.

LIZ. Yer're as tight as a flea's arse'ole.

BARRY. An 'alf as 'andsome. I know. – Out a change.

LIZ *gives him sixpence. He goes off down right.* MIKE *brings on
two cups.*

MIKE. Comin' up.

FRED. Very 'andy.

BARRY (*off*). 'Ow about 'I Broke my 'Eart'?

LIZ. Yeh. Thass great.

BARRY (*off*). Well they ain' got it.

LIZ. Funny! What about 'My 'Eart is Broken'?

MIKE (*to* LIZ). One coffee.

BARRY (*off*). They got that.

LIZ (*to* MIKE). The sugar in it?

MIKE. Taste it.

MIKE *goes off left.*

LEN. Whass it like, Fred?

FRED (*drinks*). It ain' like this in there.

LEN. Fred.

FRED. I tol' yer.

LEN. No yer ain'.

FRED. I forget.

LEN. I thought yer'd a bin full a it. I was –

FRED. Len!

LEN. – curious, thass all, 'ow it feels t' –

FRED. No!

He slams his fist on the table.

LEN. Okay.

FRED. It's finished.

LEN. Yeh.

FRED (*stands*). What yer wan' a do?

The juke box starts.

LEN. Nothin'.

FRED. Wass 'e gettin' at?

LEN. It's finished.

PETE, MIKE, COLIN *and* BARRY *come on.* PAM *stands.* LIZ
still sits.

FRED. I were'n the only one.

LEN. I ain' gettin' at yer, skip.

PETE. Wass up?

FRED. Nothin' a do with you.

PAM. 'E was rowin'.

FRED. It's nothin'. Where's that grub?

PAM. I knew 'e'd start somethin'.

FRED. Forget it.

PAM. I tol' 'im not t' come.

FRED. Where's that flippin' grub? Move.

COLIN *and* MIKE *go off left.*

PAM. 'E won't let me alone.

FRED. I'm starvin' I know that.

PAM. 'E follers me everywhere.

FRED. Ain' you lucky.

PAM. Tell 'im for me! 'It 'im! 'It 'im!

FRED. It's nothin' a do with me!

PAM. It is! It is!

BARRY. She's started.

FRED. 'Ere we go!

He sits and puts his head in his hands.

PAM (*to* LEN). See what yer done?

FRED. Didn't take 'er long.

PAM. It's your place t' stick up for me, love. I went through all that trouble for you! Somebody's got a save me from 'im.

FRED. Thanks. Thanks very much. I'll remember this.

He stands and starts back to his own table.

LIZ (*starting to click her fingers*). I can't 'ear the music!

PAM (*to* LEN). Don't bloody sit there! Yer done enough 'arm!

PETE 'Oo brought 'er 'ere?

FRED. Chriss knows!

PAM (*pointing to* LEN). 'E started this!

FRED. I don't care what bleedin' wet started it. You can stop it!

PAM (*to* LEN). I 'ate yer for this!

FRED. BELT UP!

PAM (*goes to* FRED, *who sits at his table*). I'm sorry. Fred, 'e's goin' now. It'll be all right when 'e's gone.

LEN *does not move.*

FRED. All right.

PAM (*looks round*). Where's 'is grub? 'E's starvin' 'ere. (*She goes to touch his arm.*) I get so worked up when 'e –

FRED. Keep yer 'ands off me! So 'elp me I'll land yer so bloody 'ard they'll put me back for life!

PETE (*moving in*). Right. Less get ourselves sorted out.

COLIN *comes on left.*

PAM. It don't matter. I juss got excited. (*Calls.*) Where's 'is breakfast? It'll be time for –

FRED. Breakfast? I couldn't eat in this bloody place if they served it through a rubber tube.

PETE. Come on! (*Calls.*) Mike!

FRED. All I done for 'er an' she 'as the bloody nerve t' start this!

PETE. Come on, less move.

BARRY. She wants throttlin'.

MIKE *comes on left.* COLIN *and* FRED *go out right. The door bangs.*

LIZ. I ain' drunk me coffee.

PETE. I said move!

MIKE. Flippin' mad'ouse.

MIKE *goes out right. The door bangs.*

LIZ. We paid for it!

PETE. Move!

LIZ *and* BARRY *go out right. The door bangs.*

You come near 'im again an' I'll settle yer for good. Lay off.

PETE *goes out right. The door bangs.* LEN *still sits.* PAM *stands. Pause.*

LEN. I'll see yer 'ome. I'm late for work already. I know I'm in the way. Yer can't go round the streets when yer're like that. (*He hesitates.*) They ain' done 'im no good. 'Es gone back like a kid. Yer well out a it. (*He stands.*) I knew the little bleeder 'ld do a bunk! Can't we try an' get on like before? (*He looks round.*) There's no one else. Yer only live once.

SCENE ELEVEN

The living-room.

On the table: bread, butter, breadknife, cup and saucer and milk.

MARY *sits on the couch.*

HARRY *comes in with a pot of tea. He goes to the table. He cuts and butters bread. Pause while he works.*

MARY *goes out.* HARRY *goes on working.* MARY *comes back with a cup and saucer. She pours herself tea. She takes it to the couch and sits. She sips.*

HARRY *moves so that his back is to her. He puts his cup upright in his saucer. He puts milk in the cup. He reaches to pick up the teapot.*

MARY *stands, goes to the table, and moves the teapot out of his reach. She goes back to the couch. Sits. Sips.*

MARY. My teapot.

Sips. Pause.

HARRY. My tea.

He pours tea into his cup. MARY *stands and goes to the table. She empties his cup on the floor.*

HARRY. Our'n. Weddin' present.
MARY (*goes to the couch and sits*). From *my* mother.
HARRY. That was joint.
MARY. Don't you dare talk to me!

HARRY *goes out.*

MARY (*loudly*). Some minds want boilin' in carbolic. Soap's too good for 'em. (*Slight pause.*) Dirty filth! Worse! Ha! (*She goes to the door and calls*). Don't you dare talk to me!

She goes to the couch and sits. HARRY *comes in.*

HARRY. I'll juss say one word. I saw yer with yer skirt up. Yer call me filth?

HARRY goes out. Slight pause. MARY *goes to the table and empties his slices of bread on to the floor. She goes back to the couch and drinks her tea.*

MARY. Mind out of a drain! I wouldn't let a kid like that touch me if 'e paid for it!

HARRY comes in. He goes straight to the table.

HARRY. I don't want to listen.

MARY. Filth!

HARRY. There's bin enough trouble in this 'ouse. Now yer wan'a cause trouble with 'im!

MARY. Don't talk t' me! You!

HARRY (*sees his bread on the floor*). Yer juss wan'a start trouble like there was before! (*He stoops and picks up the bread.*) Middle-age woman – goin' with 'er own daughter's left-overs – 'alf 'er age – makin' 'erself a spectacle – look at this! – No self control.

MARY. Filth!

HARRY. Like a child – I pity the lad – must want 'is 'ead tested.

MARY. There'll be some changes in this 'ouse. I ain' puttin' up with this after t'day. Yer can leave my things alone for a start. All this stuff come out a my pocket. I worked for it! I ain' 'avin' you dirtyin' me kitchin. Yer can get yerself some new towels for a start! An' plates! An' knives! An' cups! Yer'll soon find a difference!

HARRY. Don't threaten me –

MARY. An' my cooker! An' my curtains! An' my sheets!

HARRY. Yer'll say somethin' yer'll be sorry for!

He comes towards her. There is a chair in the way. He trips over it. The leg comes off.

MARY. Don't you touch me!

HARRY. Two can play at your game! Yeh! I can stop your money t'morra!

MARY. Don't yer raise yer 'and t' me!

HARRY *goes back to the table. He starts cutting bread. Pause.*

I knew yer was stood outside when 'e was there. I 'eard yer through the door. I'd a bet my life you'd come in!

HARRY. Old enough t' be 'is mother. Yer must be 'ard up!

MARY. I seen you stuck 'ere long enough! You couldn't pick an' choose!

HARRY. One was enough.

MARY. No one else would a put up with yer!

HARRY. I can do without! Yer ain' worth it!

MARY. Ha! I saw yer face when yer come through that door. I bin watchin' yer all the week. I know you of old, Harry!

HARRY. Yer'll go out a yer mind one day!

MARY. Filth!

HARRY. I 'ad enough a you in the past! I ain' puttin' up with your lark again. I'm too old. I wan' a bit a peace an' quiet.

MARY. Then why did yer come in?

HARRY. Me pools was in that table.

MARY. Yer was spyin'! Yer bin sniffin' round ever since! I ain' puttin' up with your dirt! (*She picks up the teapot.*) Yer can bloody well stay in yer room!

PAM *comes in.*

PAM. Chriss. (*Calls.*) It's them!

HARRY (*cutting bread*). I ain' sunk so low I'll bother *you*!

MARY. Yer jealous ol' swine!

HARRY. Of a bag like you?

MARY. 'E don't think so! I could a gone t'bed, an' I will next time 'e arsts me!

HARRY. Now 'e's caught a sniff a yer 'e'll be off with 'is tail between 'is legs?

She hits him with the teapot. The water pours over him. PAM *is too frightened to move.*

Ah!

MARY. 'Ope yer die!

HARRY. Blood!

MARY. Use words t' me!

HARRY. Blood!

PAM. Mum!

HARRY. Ah!

LEN (*off*). Whass up?

HARRY. Doctor.

MARY. Cracked me weddin' present. 'Im.

LEN *comes in.*

LEN. Blimey!

HARRY. Scalded!

PAM. Whass 'appenin'?

HARRY. She tried t' murder me!

MARY. Yer little liar!

PAM. Are yer all right?

HARRY. Yer saw 'er.

MARY. 'E went mad.

LEN. It's only a scratch.

PAM (*to* MARY). Why?

MARY. 'Effin an' blindin'.

LEN. Yer'll live.

HARRY. Blood.

PAM (*to* MARY). Whass 'e done?

LEN. 'E's all wet.

MARY. Swore at me!

PAM. Why?

HARRY. Doctor.

MARY. There's nothin' wrong with 'im.

HARRY. Scalded.

MARY. I 'ardly touched 'im. 'E needs a good thrashin'!

LEN (*to* PAM). Get a towel.

HARRY. I ain' allowed t' touch the towels.

MARY. I kep' this twenty-three years. Look what 'e's done to it!

PAM. *What 'appened?*

LEN. Nothin'. They 'ad a row.

PAM. 'E called 'er a bag.

LEN. It's nothin'. I'd better be off t' work. They'll give us me cards. We juss seen Fred. 'E looks all right, well 'e don't look bad. It ain' Butlins. (*To* PAM.) Get 'im up t' bed. Put the kettle on. Yer could all do with a cup a tea.

PAM (*to* MARY). What made yer start talkin'?

MARY. Yer 'eard 'im call me a bag. (*To* LEN.) 'E went mad over catchin' you last week.

LEN (*looking at* HARRY's *head*). Yer'll 'ave t' wash that cut. It's got tealeaves in it.

HARRY *dabs at it with the tail of his shirt.*

PAM. Caught 'oo last week?

MARY (*pointing to* HARRY). 'Is filth. (*Points to* LEN.) Arst 'im!

PAM (*to* LEN). What 'appened?

LEN. Nothin'.

HARRY. I was cuttin' bread. (*He picks up the knife.*) She flew at me!

PAM (*to* LEN). I knew it was you! (*To* HARRY.) Whass 'e done?

LEN. Nothin'.

MARY. Filth!

HARRY. I found 'em both.

He points with the knife to the spot.

LEN (*pulling at* HARRY). No!

HARRY. She'll 'ave t' 'ear.

LEN (*he pulls at him*). No!

HARRY. She 'ad 'er clothes up.

PAM. No!

LEN. Yer bloody fool! Yer bloody, bloody fool!

LEN *shakes* HARRY. *The knife waves through the air.*

HARRY. Ah!

PAM. That knife!

MARY. Filth!

PAM. 'E'll kill 'im!

LEN. Bloody fool.

PAM (*screams*). Oh! No! – Whass 'appenin' to us?

She sits on the couch and cries. Pause.

HARRY. 'Im an' 'er.

PAM (*crying*). Why don't 'e go? Why don't 'e go away? All my friends gone. Baby's gone. Nothin' left but rows. Day in, day out. Fightin' with knives.

HARRY. I'm shakin'.

PAM (*crying*). They'll kill each other soon.

LEN (*to* PAM). Yer can't blame them on me!

PAM (*crying*). Why can't 'e go away!

HARRY (*removes his shirt*). Wet.

PAM (*crying*). Look at me. I can't sleep with worry.

MARY. Breakin' me 'ome.

PAM (*crying*). 'E's killed me baby. Taken me friends. Broken me 'ome.

HARRY. More blood.

MARY. I ain' clearin' up after 'im. 'E can clear 'is own mess.

PAM (*crying*). I can't go on like this.

LEN (*to* PAM). There was nothin' in it!

PAM (*crying*). I'll throw myself somewhere. It's the only way.

HARRY. Cold.

LEN *goes to* HARRY.

PAM (*sitting and crying*). Stop 'im! They'll kill each other!

LEN (*stops*). I was goin' a 'elp 'im.

PAM (*crying*). Take that knife. The baby's dead. They're all gone. It's the only way. I can't go on.

MARY. Next time 'e won't be so lucky.

PAM (*crying*). Yer can't call it livin'. 'E's pullin' me t' pieces. Nothin' but trouble.

LEN. I'm tryin' t' 'elp! 'Oo else'll 'elp? If I go will they come back? Will the baby come back? Will 'e come back? I'm the only one that's stayed an' yer wan'a get rid a me!

PAM (*crying*). I can't stand any more. Baby dead. No friends.

LEN. I'll go.

PAM (*crying*). No one listens. Why don't 'e go? Why don't they make 'im go?

MARY. 'E can stay in 'is own room after t'day.

LEN. I'll find somewhere dinnertime.

HARRY. Me neck's throbbin'.

PAM (*crying*). No 'ome. No friends. Baby dead. Gone. Fred gone.

SCENE TWELVE

LEN's *bedroom.*

LEN *lies face down on the floor. The side of his face is flat against the floorboards. He holds a knife. There is an open suitcase on the bed. In it are a few things. Pause.*

The door opens. HARRY *comes in. He wears long white combinations. He wears pale socks. No shoes. His head is in a skull cap of bandages. He comes up behind* LEN. LEN *sees him slowly.*

HARRY. Evenin'.

LEN. Evenin'.

HARRY. Get up. Yer'll catch cold down there.

LEN. 'Ow's yer 'ead?

HARRY (*touches it*). Don't know.

LEN. Thass a good sign.

HARRY. All right now?

LEN. I was listenin'.

He draws the knife between two boards.

Clears the crack. Yer can 'ear better.

HARRY. Thass a good knife.

LEN. She's got someone with 'er.

HARRY. Thought yer might like someone t' say good night.

LEN. Yer can 'ear 'er voice.

HARRY. No.

LEN. She's picked someone up. I couldn't get anywhere with me packin'.

HARRY. No, I saw 'er come in.

LEN. Could a swore I 'eard someone.

HARRY. Not with 'er!

LEN. She's still good lookin'.

HARRY. 'Er sort's two a penny. Lads don't 'ave t' put up with 'er carry-on.

LEN. I used t' 'ear Fred an' her down there.

HARRY. No more.

LEN. Kep' me awake.

HARRY (*sits on the bed*). Tired. Nice 'ere.

LEN. Seen worse.

HARRY. Quiet.

LEN. Sometimes.

Pause.

HARRY. She's cryin'.

LEN. O.

HARRY. In bed. I passed 'er door.

LEN. I knew I 'eard somethin'.

HARRY. Thass what yer 'eard.

LEN *puts a pair of socks in the case.*

Won't be the last time.

LEN. Eh?

HARRY. 'Owlin in bed.

LEN. O.

HARRY. She'll pay for it.

LEN. What?

HARRY. 'Er ways. Yer'll get yer own back.

LEN. I lost me case keys.

HARRY. Yer'll see.

LEN. Long time since I used it.

HARRY. Where yer goin'?

LEN. 'Ad enough.

HARRY. No different any other place.

LEN. I've heard it all before.

Pause.

HARRY. Thought yer'd like t' say good night.

LEN. Yeh. Ta.

HARRY. They're all in bed.

LEN. I get in the way, don't I?

HARRY. Take no notice.

LEN. Sick a rows.

HARRY. They've 'ad their say. They'll keep quiet now.

LEN. I upset every –

HARRY. No different if yer go. They won't let yer drop.

LEN. Different for me.

He puts a shirt in the case.

I never put a finger on your ol' woman. I juss give 'er a 'and.

HARRY. I known 'er longer'n you.

LEN. She reckoned she was late.

HARRY. Ain' my worry.

LEN. But yer 'ad a row.

HARRY. She 'ad a row.

LEN. You shouted.

HARRY. It ain' like that.

LEN. I 'eard yer.

HARRY. It clears the air. Sometimes. It's finished. – You shouted.

Pause.

LEN. I'll 'ave t' look for that key.

HARRY. I left 'er once.

LEN. You?

HARRY. I come back.

LEN. Why?

HARRY. I worked it out. Why should I soil me 'ands washin' an' cookin'? Let 'er do it. She'll find out.

LEN. Yer do yer own washin'.

HARRY. Eh?

LEN. An' cookin'.

HARRY. Ah, *now.*

Pause.

LEN. I can do without the key. I ain' goin' far.

HARRY. Bin in the army?

LEN. No.

HARRY. Yer can see that. Know where yer goin'?

LEN. Someplace 'andy. For work.

HARRY. Round Fred?

LEN. No.

HARRY. She won't see 'im again.

LEN. Best thing, too. Yer ain' seen what it done t' 'im. 'E's like a kid. 'E'll finished up like some ol' lag, or an' ol' soak. Bound to. An' soon. Yer'll see.

He moves the case along the bed.

That'll keep till t'morrow.

HARRY. It's a shame.

LEN. Too tired t'night. Wass a shame?

HARRY. Yer stood all the rows. Now it'll settle down an' yer –

LEN. I 'ad my last row, I know that.

HARRY. Sit 'ere.

LEN (*sits on the bed*). It's bin a 'ard day.

HARRY. Finished now.

A long pause.

LEN. I'd like t' get up t'morrow mornin' and clear right out.
There's nothin' t' keep me 'ere. What do I get out a it?
Jack it in. Emigrate.

HARRY. Yer're too young t' emigrate. Do that when yer past
fifty.

LEN. I don't give a damn if they don't talk, but they don't even
listen t' yer. Why the 'ell should I bother about 'er?

HARRY. It's juss a rough patch. We 'ad t' sort ourselves out
when you joined us. But yer fit in now. It'll settle down.

LEN. No one tells yer anything really.

Slight pause.

Was she all right?

HARRY. Eh?

LEN. In bed.

HARRY. Yer know.

LEN. No.

HARRY. Up t' the man.

LEN. Yeh?

HARRY. I 'ad the best.

LEN. Go on.

HARRY (*quietly*). I 'ad 'er squealing like a pig.

LEN. Yeh.

HARRY. There was a little boy first.

LEN. In the war.

HARRY. Then the girl.

LEN. On leave.

HARRY. An' back t' the front.

LEN. Go on.

HARRY. I saw the lot.

LEN. What was it like?

HARRY. War?

Slight pause.

Most I remember the peace an' quiet. Once or twice the 'ole lot blew up. Not more. Then it went quiet. Everythin' still. Yer don't get it that quiet now.

LEN. Not 'ere.

HARRY. Nowhere.

LEN. Kill anyone?

HARRY. Must 'ave. Yer never saw the bleeders, 'ceptin' prisoners or dead. Well, I did once. I was in a room. Some bloke stood up in the door. Lost, I expect. I shot 'im. 'E fell down. Like a coat fallin' off a 'anger, I always say. Not a word.

Pause.

Yer never killed yer man. Yer missed that. Gives yer a sense a perspective. I was one a the lucky ones.

Pause.

LEN. 'Oo tied your 'ead?

HARRY. I managed. I never arst them.

LEN. I'm good at that.

HARRY. No need.

Pause.

Nigh on midnight.

LEN. Gone.

He takes off his shoes and stands. He drops his trousers.

HARRY. Yer don't wan'a go.

LEN. Eh?

HARRY. Don't go. No point.

LEN (*his trousers round his ankles*). Why?

HARRY. Yer'd come back.

LEN. No use sayin' anythin' t'night –

HARRY. Don't let 'em push yer out.

LEN. Depends 'ow I feel in the mornin'.

He sits on the bed and pulls off his trousers.

HARRY. Choose yer own time. Not when it suits them.

LEN. I don't know anythin' t'night.

HARRY. I'd like yer t' stay. If yer can see yer way to.

LEN. Why?

HARRY (*after a slight pause*). I ain' stayin'.

LEN. What?

HARRY. Not always.

LEN. O, yeh.

He puts the case on the floor.

HARRY. Yer'll see. If I was t' go now she'd be laughin'. She'd soon 'ave someone in my bed. She knows 'ow t' be'ave when she likes. An' cook.

LEN. Yeh, yeh.

He slides the case under the bed and sits on the bed.

HARRY. I'll go when I'm ready. When she's on 'er pension. She won't get no one after 'er then. I'll be *out*. Then see 'ow she copes.

LEN. Ain' worth it, pop.

HARRY. It's only right. When someone carries on like 'er, they 'ave t' pay for it. People can't get away with murder. What 'd 'appen then?

LEN. Don't arst me.

HARRY. She thinks she's on top. I'll 'ave t' fall back a bit – buy a few things an' stay in me room more. I can wait.

LEN. 'Ead still 'urt?

HARRY. She'll find out.

LEN. I can let yer 'ave some aspirins.

HARRY. Eh?

LEN. Can yer move up.

Harry stands.

No, I didn't mean that.

HARRY. Yer should be in bed. We don't wan'a waste the light.

LEN. I won't let on what yer said.

HARRY. Eh?

LEN. You leavin'.

HARRY. She knows.

LEN. Yer told 'er?

HARRY. We don't 'ave secrets. They make trouble.

He goes to the door.

Don't speak to 'em at all. It saves a lot a misunderstandin'.

LEN. O.

HARRY. Yer'll be all right in the mornin'.

LEN. No work t'night?

HARRY. Saturday.

LEN. I forgot.

HARRY. Night.

LEN. Funny we never talked before.

HARRY. They listen all the time.

LEN. Will yer come up next Saturday night?

HARRY. No, no. Cause trouble. They won't stand for it.

LEN. I'd like t' tell 'er t' jump off once more.

HARRY. Sometime. Don't upset 'er. It ain' fair. Thass best all round.

LEN (*looks round*). It's like that.

HARRY. Listen!

LEN. What?

HARRY *holds up his hand. Silence.*

Still cryin'?

HARRY. She's gone quiet.

Silence.

There – she's movin'.

Silence.

LEN. She's 'eard us.

HARRY. Best keep away, yer see. Good night.
LEN. But –
HARRY. Sh!

He holds up his hand again. They listen. Silence. Pause.

HARRY. Good night.
LEN. 'Night.

HARRY *goes.*

SCENE THIRTEEN

The living-room.

PAM *sits on the couch. She reads the* Radio Times.

MARY *takes things from the table and goes out. Pause. She comes back. She goes to the table. She collects the plates. She goes out.*

Pause. The door opens. HARRY *comes in. He goes to the table and opens the drawer. He searches in it.*

PAM *turns a page.*

MARY *comes in. She goes to the table and picks up the last things on it. She goes out.*

HARRY'S *jacket is draped on the back of the chair by the table. He searches in the pockets.*

PAM *turns a page.*

There is a loud bang (off).

Silence.

HARRY *turns to the table and searches in the drawer.*

MARY *comes in. She wipes the table top with a damp cloth.*

There is a loud bang (off).

MARY *goes out.*

HARRY *takes ink and envelope out of the drawer. He puts them on the table. He sits on the chair. He feels behind him and takes a pen from the inside pocket of his jacket. He starts to fill in his football coupon.*

A short silence.

PAM *quickly turns over two pages.*

Immediately the door opens and LEN *comes in. He carries the chair that* HARRY *tripped over and broke. He takes it down right and sets it on the floor. He crouches. His head is below the level of the seat. He looks under the chair. He turns it upside down. He fiddles with the loose leg.*

MARY *comes in. She straightens the couch. She takes off her apron and folds it neatly. She sits on the couch and pushes the apron down the side of the couch.*

Silence.

Stop.

LEN *turns the chair upright. He still crouches. He rests his left wrist high on the chair back and his right elbow on the chair seat. His right hand hangs in space. His back is to the audience. His head is sunk into his shoulders. He thinks for a moment.*

PAM *stands and goes to the door.*

LEN. Fetch me 'ammer.

PAM *goes out.* HARRY *writes.* MARY *sits.* LEN *presses his hand on the seat and the chair wobbles.* MARY *takes up the* Radio Times *and glances at the back page.* HARRY *takes a small leather folder out of the inside pocket of his jacket. He places the folder on the table.*

PAM *comes in and sits on the couch.*

LEN *turns the chair upside down and looks at it.*

MARY *puts the* Radio Times *back on the couch. She pats the pillow.* PAM *picks up the* Radio Times. *In one connected movement* LEN *turns the chair upright and stands to his full height. He has grasped the seat at diagonally opposite corners, so that the diagonal is parallel with the front of his body. He brings the chair sharply down so that the foot furthest from him strikes the floor first. It makes a loud bang. Still standing upright he turns the chair upside down and looks at the leg. He turns the chair upright and sets it down. He crouches. He places the flat of his palm on the seat. The chair still has a little wobble.*

PAM *folds the* Radio Times *and puts it down.*

HARRY *takes a stamp from the folder.* LEN *sits on the chair and faces front. He puts his head between his knees to peer under the chair.* HARRY *licks the stamp and silently stamps the envelope. He reaches behind him and puts the folder and the spare coupon in the inside pocket of his jacket.*

LEN *gets off the chair and crouches beside it. His back is to the audience. He bends over the chair so that his stomach or chest rests on the seat. He reaches down with his left hand and pulls the loose rear leg up into the socket.*

HARRY *reaches behind him and puts his pen into the breast pocket of his jacket. He puts the ink in the table drawer.*

LEN *slips his left arm round the back of the chair. His chest rests against the side edge of the seat. The fingers of his right hand touch the floor. His head lies sideways on the seat.*

MARY *sits.* PAM *sits.*

HARRY *licks the flap on the envelope and closes it quietly.*

The curtain falls quickly.

A SELECTED LIST OF
METHUEN MODERN PLAYS

☐	ANTIGONE	Jean Anouilh	£6.99
☐	THE HOSTAGE	Brendan Behan	£6.99
☐	SAVED	Edward Bond	£6.99
☐	MOTHER COURAGE	Bertolt Brecht	£6.99
☐	THE CAUCASIAN CHALK CIRCLE	Bertolt Brecht	£6.99
☐	THE RESISTIBLE RISE OF ARTURO UI	Bertolt Brecht	£6.99
☐	THE THREEPENNY OPERA	Bertolt Brecht	£6.99
☐	THE GOOD PERSON OF SZECHWAN	Bertolt Brecht	£7.99
☐	PRIVATE LIVES	Noël Coward	£6.99
☐	A TASTE OF HONEY	Shelagh Delaney	£6.99
☐	LOOT	Joe Orton	£6.99
☐	WHAT THE BUTLER SAW	Joe Orton	£6.99
☐	OH WHAT A LOVELY WAR	Theatre Workshop	£6.99

• All Methuen Drama books are available through mail order or from your local bookshop.

Please send cheque/eurocheque/postal order (sterling only) Access, Visa, Mastercard, Diners Card, Switch or Amex.

☐☐☐☐☐☐☐☐☐☐☐☐☐☐☐☐

Expiry Date: _____ Signature: _____

UK customers please allow £1 for the first book and 50p thereafter up to a maximum of £3 for postage and packing. Overseas customers please allow £1.50 for the first book and 75p thereafter up to a maximum of £5 for post and packing.

ALL ORDERS TO:

Methuen Books, Books by Post, TBS Limited, The Book Service, Colchester Road, Frating Green, Colchester, Essex CO7 7DW.

NAME: _____

ADDRESS: _____

_____

Please allow 28 days for delivery. Please tick box if you do not wish to receive any additional information   ☐

Prices and availability subject to change without notice.

Methuen Modern Plays
include work by

Jean Anouilh
John Arden
Margaretta D'Arcy
Peter Barnes
Sebastian Barry
Brendan Behan
Dermot Bolger
Edward Bond
Bertolt Brecht
Howard Brenton
Anthony Burgess
Simon Burke
Jim Cartwright
Caryl Churchill
Noël Coward
Lucinda Coxon
Sarah Daniels
Nick Darke
Nick Dear
Shelagh Delaney
David Edgar
David Eldridge
Dario Fo
Michael Frayn
John Godber
Paul Godfrey
David Greig
John Guare
Peter Handke
David Harrower
Jonathan Harvey
Iain Heggie
Declan Hughes
Terry Johnson
Sarah Kane
Charlotte Keatley
Barrie Keeffe
Howard Korder

Robert Lepage
Stephen Lowe
Doug Lucie
Martin McDonagh
John McGrath
Terrence McNally
David Mamet
Patrick Marber
Arthur Miller
Mtwa, Ngema & Simon
Tom Murphy
Phyllis Nagy
Peter Nichols
Joseph O'Connor
Joe Orton
Louise Page
Joe Penhall
Luigi Pirandello
Stephen Poliakoff
Franca Rame
Mark Ravenhill
Philip Ridley
Reginald Rose
David Rudkin
Willy Russell
Jean-Paul Sartre
Sam Shepard
Wole Soyinka
Shelagh Stephenson
C. P. Taylor
Theatre de Complicite
Theatre Workshop
Sue Townsend
Judy Upton
Timberlake Wertenbaker
Roy Williams
Victoria Wood